WORLD WAR II HISTORY FOR TEENS

WORLD WAR II HISTORY

★ FOR TEENS ★

Understanding the Major Battles, Military Strategy, and Arc of War

Benjamin Mack-Jackson

callisto
publishing
an imprint of Sourcebooks

Copyright © 2021 by Callisto Publishing LLC
Cover and internal design © 2021 by Callisto Publishing LLC
Photography used under license from Alamy. Illustrations used under license from Creative Market.
Interior and Cover Designer: Erin Yeung
Art Producer: Sara Feinstein
Editor: Barbara J. Isenberg
Production Manager: Martin Worthington
Production Editor: Sigi Nacson

Published by Callisto Publishing LLC C/O Sourcebooks LLC
P.O. Box 4410, Naperville, Illinois 60567-4410
(630) 961-3900
callistopublishing.com

Printed in the United States of America
SB 2

Dedicated to the World War II veterans, our nation's greatest generation, and the future generations who have the responsibility to remember the past.

CONTENTS

CHAPTER 3
GERMANY MOVES EAST 33

CHAPTER 4
THE PACIFIC THEATER 51

CHAPTER 8

AFTERMATH AND IMPACT 125

INTRODUCTION

History matters. Whether you've heard this phrase before or not, it will set the tone for the events covered in this book and how they connect to the modern world. When you think of World War II, you may think of record players, black-and-white movies, and a world without cell phones or computers. But studying this defining period in history can actually teach you a lot about today. History is more than just a study of our past. Understanding history helps us discover where we came from, avoid past mistakes, and learn how to build a better future.

I discovered the importance of history at a young age. When I was 13 years old, I embarked on a journey to expand my knowledge of World War II by talking to those who lived through it. What started as a personal endeavor has transformed into the WWII Veterans History Project, a nonprofit dedicated to preserving the memories of World War II veterans for future generations. Studying and sharing the stories of World War II has become more than a passion. It is my life's mission—a mission that has taken me across the United States and the world, capturing and preserving endless stories along the way. My experiences have led me to understand truly how much history matters.

Understanding the full story of World War II can be complicated and confusing. For almost six years, nearly every country on Earth participated in arguably the largest and deadliest conflict the world has ever seen. Fighting took place on the continents of Africa, Asia, and Europe, as well as at sea. An estimated 75 million people perished, approximately 3 percent of the world's population. Ethnic groups were massacred, leading to new terms such as *genocide* and *crimes against humanity*.

But amid the destruction, the world was building the foundation for its future. Entire societies participated in the fight to free the world from tyranny and invested in the future of their countries. World War II united people like never before, leading to rapid technological advancements and laying the foundation for global partnerships such as NATO and the United Nations. Simply put, World War II built the world that we know today.

This book serves to tell the story of World War II and some of its greatest battles. And while it is a thorough record of the war, it is far from the full story. To this day, historians are still discovering new things about the war. The scale and magnitude was unlike anything that came before it, making World War II the single most defining moment of the 20th century. It influenced everything from politics to culture, fashion to language, and everything in between. But the most important reminder of the war that exists today are the few remaining survivors who can shed a unique light on what life was really like during those distressing times.

I've used my experiences and lessons from more than 100 interviews with World War II veterans and eyewitnesses as the primary motivation to write this book. While their individual stories are not directly featured, these unique opportunities made me understand the importance of keeping the story of World War II alive. As the last survivors leave us, it is more important than ever that the story of World War II is passed on for generations to come.

As you read on, I hope you will gain not only an understanding of the history but also an appreciation for the men and women who actually lived through it. We can learn a lot from our past, especially how much our nation—and our world—rose from the war's ashes. As renowned philosopher George Santayana once said, "Those who cannot remember the past are condemned to repeat it." If this book teaches you only one thing, it should be that a war as destructive as World War II is something we cannot afford to repeat.

CHAPTER 1

PRELUDE TO WORLD WAR II

To fully understand the story of World War II, one needs to learn what took place before the start of the conflict. Two decades of turmoil and unrest across the globe paved the way for the events that followed. This chapter will introduce the countries, leaders, and major decisions that led to the start of World War II.

Between the Wars

World War II began in 1939, but to comprehend the full story
we must go back to 1918. We have to explore how World War I
and its aftermath set the stage for another global conflict. In
1918, "the war to end all wars" came to a close. After four long
years of conflict and much destruction, the world vowed never
to make war again. In order to resolve world issues before
they led to war, the League of Nations was formed. The league
served as an innovative way for independent nations to negotiate peacefully in an open forum. However, the weakness of
the organization soon became apparent, and its ineffectiveness
led to chaos.

Throughout the 1920s and '30s, European politics became
sharply divided as right-wing and left-wing movements
gained power. German history provides perhaps the clear-
est example. The Treaty of Versailles, which officially ended
World War I, was incredibly harsh toward Germany. It forced
the country to accept full responsibility for the war and pay
a large sum of money, called reparations. This ruined the
already wounded German economy and led to total chaos in
the government.

Meanwhile, in southern Europe, Italy's economy was in a
similar position: unemployment was on the rise, workers were
going on strike, and inflation ravaged the economy. In both
Germany and Italy, the people looked to far-right politicians
for answers. They adopted fascist (authoritarian) governments
that ruled with an iron fist.

To the east, Russia had opted for far-left politics. After a
violent revolution in 1917 and a resulting civil war that ended
in the 1920s, communists were in control of the entire country, and the Soviet Union was established. Farther east, the
Japanese adopted a powerful authoritarian government controlled by the military. As Japan's war machine and economy

surged, its hunger for natural resources and territorial expansion led to heightened tensions around the Pacific.

With all these mounting tensions, Britain and France strengthened their defensive positions and watched as the global situation unfolded. They planned to keep Europe at peace through appeasement, by trying to meet the various demands of adversaries. The United States, however, chose a strict policy of isolationism to distance itself from foreign affairs. Following World War I—or the "Great War," as it was called at the time—America enjoyed a period of peace and prosperity. All of that changed with the stock market crash of 1929. The Great Depression that followed had a severe economic impact on almost every nation. The extremist nature of world politics, combined with renewed economic disparity, set the stage for war.

Germany: The Rise of the Nazi Party

On November 11, 1918, Germany signed an armistice (an agreement to stop fighting) with the Allied powers—Great Britain, France, and Russia—that ended World War I. While this came as a relief to many, much of Germany's population didn't share the positive spirit. They felt that victory had been within their reach and that corrupt politicians had backstabbed the military. To add to these internal disputes, the Allies imposed the harsh Treaty of Versailles. As part of the agreement, the Allies forced the Germans to give up large amounts of land, dismantle its military, and pay substantial reparations. The terms were humiliating to Germany and crippled their economy.

In 1919, Adolf Hitler, a native-born Austrian, was a recently discharged Bavarian army veteran. Hitler, like most Germans, was frustrated by defeat in the war. He joined an emerging right-wing political party called the National Socialist German Workers' Party, commonly referred to as the Nazi Party.

Hitler quickly rose to become one of its most popular and respected members. The Nazis condemned both communism and capitalism, calling them international Jewish conspiracies to destroy Germany. Of course, these claims were completely false, but Hitler found great success playing on Germans' fears. His popular and fiery anti-Semitic speeches offered people someone to blame their troubles on.

THE REICHSTAG BUILDING ABLAZE IN BERLIN, FEBRUARY 1933

In 1923, the Nazis made an unsuccessful attempt to seize power in Germany through a violent revolution. Hitler was put in prison for treason, and the Nazi Party was banned. A year later he was released and immediately began rebuilding

the movement. In 1929, the Great Depression swept across
Germany, which led to a new wave of support for the Nazis.
In such a desperate atmosphere, the people of Germany
once again searched for answers. They found them in Adolf
Hitler. Hitler ran for president in 1932 but lost the election to
a decorated war hero named General Paul von Hindenburg.
Although he had not achieved victory, Hitler won more than
36 percent of the vote. Since no party held a majority in the
Reichstag, in order to form a coalition government, Hinden-
burg appointed Hitler chancellor. Therefore, in 1933, Adolf
Hitler became the second most powerful man in Germany.
When Hindenburg died in 1934, Hitler merged the roles of
president and chancellor, proclaiming himself "Führer," the

supreme leader of the country. Further, he called his regime the "Third Reich" ("Third Empire"), referring back to the two great German empires that had come before. Under Hitler's regime, Germany began a secret military buildup, recruiting large numbers of troops, organizing a modern air force, and building a massive fleet of warships. The German economy surged, and millions of new jobs were created. Hitler and the Nazis became more popular than ever.

Italy: Fascism Takes Over

Much like Germany, Italy faced high unemployment, inflation, and a fear of communist influence in politics during the years following World War I. (In both countries, communists were seen as unpatriotic.) In 1919, Italian war veteran and aspiring journalist Benito Mussolini formed the Fascist Party. This new political movement rapidly drew the support of thousands. Appealing to the wounded pride of Italians frustrated by their loss in World War I, Mussolini promised to end economic suffering and eliminate the threat of communism. His persuasive speeches, combined with the glorification of the Roman Empire, stirred public emotion and made the Fascist movement immensely popular. In October 1922, amid political chaos in Italy, Mussolini led as many as 30,000 of his followers in the March on Rome, intending to force Italian king Victor Emmanuel III to concede the government. When the police and military refused to stop the movement, the king invited the Fascists to lead the nation. Once in power, Mussolini gradually eliminated Italy's democratic processes. In 1925, he declared himself dictator of Italy, taking the title "Il Duce." His regime would last for the next 20 years.

BENITO MUSSOLINI TAKES A SALUTE NEXT TO ADOLF HITLER IN
MUNICH, 1940

Fascism became a way of life for the Italian people, domi-
nating every aspect of society. Children wore black uniforms
to school and were taught absolute obedience to the government. Under Mussolini, the Italian economy drastically
improved. The transportation system was modernized, unemployment hit an all-time low, and inflation was eliminated.
Yet much of the success emerged from the fact that Mussolini
silenced all of his opposition. Rival political parties were
banned, and the Italian media became a propaganda machine.
Corresponding with his idea of a new Roman Empire,
Mussolini also believed it was the duty of powerful nations to

conquer weaker ones. Since the Italian armed forces were far from modern, Mussolini chose his enemies carefully.

In 1935, Italy invaded the small African nation of Abyssinia (now Ethiopia). Up against an army of tribesmen armed only with spears, Italian forces dropped bombs and used poison gas, acts that alarmed many European nations. Haile Selassie, the emperor of Abyssinia, pleaded with the League of Nations for support but was given no military assistance. Both Abyssinia and Italy were members of the league, yet the organization failed to take any action. In 1936, Nazi Germany and Italy signed an agreement to link as political and military allies. Mussolini famously declared that all European countries would rotate on a Rome-Berlin axis. Because Italian Fascism and Nazism shared similar ideals, it seemed natural for the two dictators to join forces. Japan would later join as well, seeking to pursue its own expansionism in the Far East. The alliance would come to be known as the Axis powers.

Japan: The Path to Military Dictatorship

As nationalist governments rose to power in Europe, a new threat was growing in the Far East. Over time, traditional Japanese imperialism had faded, and by the 1920s, Japan started to embrace some aspects of democracy in its government. Japan experienced great economic success following World War I, and many believed that democracy was the path to prosperity.

Much of Japan's financial success stemmed from exporting luxury products, such as silk, in exchange for essentials like coal and oil. But with the onset of the Great Depression in 1929, Japan's silk market crashed, leading to immense suffering across the country. Millions of Japanese faced starvation, and the economy collapsed. Radical nationalists felt that the adoption of Western democratic principles had led to the economic decline, while military leaders argued that the problems were the result of a lack of space and resources. High-ranking army officers suggested expanding into a section of China known as Manchuria, a vast resource-rich territory.

In 1931, Japanese troops sabotaged a section of their own railway that ran through Manchuria. Japan then claimed the sabotage was an act of aggression by the Chinese, thus manufacturing a justification to invade China. Within months, Manchuria was a colony of Japan, becoming its prime source for iron, steel, and coal. It also offered land for farming and room to colonize. But above all else, Manchuria gave Japan the necessary resources to build up a military to rival any Western power's. After their success in Manchuria, Japan's military leaders rapidly took control of the Japanese government, effectively establishing a military dictatorship.

Six years later, in 1937, Japan continued its conquests in Asia, invading the rest of China in a swift campaign. Upon capturing several large cities, Japanese troops brutalized the Chinese population. When Japanese forces seized Nanking, China's capital, they burned the city to the ground and committed systematic atrocities against civilians. In what became known as the "Rape of Nanking," the Japanese murdered an estimated 150,000 male prisoners of war, massacred an additional 50,000 male civilians, and raped between 20,000 and 80,000 women and girls, many of whom were killed. Helpless against the Japanese onslaught, the Chinese pleaded to the League of Nations for assistance. Although 42 of the 44 nations in the league condemned Japan's aggression, the Japanese refused to back down. The campaign in China continued, and the ineffectiveness of the league was demonstrated once more.

The United States: The Attempt to Remain Neutral

In the late 1930s, with tensions mounting in Europe and Asia, isolationism—the idea of keeping the United States out of war—was the prevailing attitude across America. When the United States entered World War I in 1917, the decision was unpopular with most Americans. They felt that the United States had minimal interest in the conflict and that sending troops overseas was unjustified. Resentment grew as the casualties increased, contributing to the isolationist platform. Immediately following World War I, Congress rejected membership in the League of Nations, concerned that it would draw the United States into another European conflict. At a time when many felt the sacrifices made during World War I were unnecessary, the possibility of entanglement in another foreign war was out of the question. Economic growth and widespread prosperity defined much of the 1920s as the country recovered from the wartime devastation.

When the Great Depression ravaged the United States in 1929, international affairs were the last thing Americans were worried about. The stock market crash and the years of financial uncertainty that followed ultimately solidified the nation's isolationist stance. During the 1930s, President Franklin Roosevelt believed that many of the United States' internal issues could be solved through a strong international agenda. But his vision on foreign policy was limited by the strength of isolationist opinion in Congress. Without the support of Congress, Roosevelt and the United States stood alone, resisting foreign involvement unless American interests were directly affected. The U.S. military was weak and ill-prepared, and politicians and military leaders alike ignored the increasing signs of future conflict. Yet, the mounting international unrest posed a dangerous threat to U.S. isolationism. Japan's occupation of Manchuria and Italy's invasion of Abyssinia, as well as Nazi Germany's annexation of Czechoslovakia in 1938, led the U.S. Congress to pass a series of neutrality acts. This legislation was designed to reassert America's neutral position to the world. Despite the troubling developments in Europe and Asia, the United States remained against direct involvement in any foreign wars.

The Soviet Union and Germany: An Unlikely Alliance

For Hitler in Germany, absolute power over a nation that adored him wasn't enough. He sought *Lebensraum* ("living space") for Germans beyond the Reich's borders. The Treaty of Versailles had forced Germany to hand over large amounts of its territory, and Hitler promised to bring all ethnic Germans back to the fatherland. When he threatened to invade Czechoslovakia to reabsorb their German-speaking population, the world took notice.

In September of 1938, at the Munich Conference, the leaders of Britain, France, and Italy agreed to allow Germany to annex the Sudetenland, a region of Czechoslovakia inhabited by German-speaking people outside the Reich. However, Germany was prohibited from any further territorial conquests. Nonetheless, when Hitler's troops marched into Austria in 1938, claiming that the majority of Austrians supported annexation, the world turned a blind eye. By allowing Hitler to incorporate the Sudetenland and Austria into the German Reich, Europe hoped to avoid another conflict. But five months later, in March of 1939, Hitler violated the agreement and invaded the remainder of Czechoslovakia. Still, the world stood by and watched, hesitant to start a war.

MATTER OF CHOICE: CHAMBERLAIN'S APPEASEMENT POLICY

In September 1938, British prime minister Neville Chamberlain returned from Germany after the Munich Conference, declaring that he had secured "peace in our time." The agreement was well received. Chamberlain's policy of appeasement would allow Europe to remain at peace. But when Hitler breached the pact just five and a half months later, the world saw his true intentions. It was apparent that appeasement had done nothing but allow Hitler to prepare his war machine unchecked. The Munich Conference was a disaster for Britain and France. It was also an immense embarrassment for Chamberlain, resulting in his eventual resignation.

Since taking power, Hitler had his sights set on invading Poland, Germany's neighbor to the east. After more than a century of foreign rule, Poland regained its independence at the end of World War I. Much of the territory Germany lost in the Treaty of Versailles made up Poland's western half. Thousands of ethnic Germans lived inside Poland's borders. Britain and France realized that Hitler intended to occupy Poland, and they pledged to defend the Poles in the event of German aggression. This worried Hitler's generals. With Britain and France to the west and the Soviet Union to the east, an attack on Poland could easily result in a two-front war.

SIGNING THE MOLOTOV-RIBBENTROP PACT, 1939

In August 1939, the world was shocked when German foreign minister Joachim von Ribbentrop flew to Moscow and signed a nonaggression pact with Soviet foreign minister Vyacheslav Molotov. The secret terms of the Molotov-Ribbentrop Pact called for Poland to be divided in half: Germany would invade the west while Soviet forces occupied the east. Because of their differing ideologies, Germany and the Soviet Union were unlikely allies. But the Molotov-Ribbentrop Pact proved beneficial to both nations. Unbeknownst to the world, Germany could now invade Poland without fear of a two-front war, and the Soviet Union was free to add more territory to its communist realm. On September 1, 1939, Germany unleashed its armies on Poland, and the world was once again at war.

ARMS AND ARMOR: THE GERMAN LUFTWAFFE

Under the terms of the Treaty of Versailles, Germany was forbidden to have an air force. But when Hitler took power in 1933, he vowed to rebuild the German military, including an ultramodern fleet of aircraft. In violation of the treaty, German pilots were trained in secret, and massive squadrons of planes were built in factories across the Third Reich. This came to be known as the "Luftwaffe." By the time war broke out in 1939, it was one of the largest and most formidable air forces in the world.

CHAPTER 2

THE GERMAN CONQUEST OF EUROPE

When the German army marched on western Europe in 1939 and 1940, it appeared unstoppable. The world watched as nation after nation fell into Hitler's sphere of influence. The decisive successes and critical failures in the first few months of World War II defined the rest of the conflict.

A New Philosophy

In the early days of World War II, much of Germany's success was attributed to blitzkrieg. This new form of war strategy led the Nazi armies to victory over nearly all of Europe in just over a year. But how was this new military tactic so successful? Blitzkrieg in German translates to "lightning war," and as the name suggests, the tactic relied heavily on shock and speed. The German military leaders developed and perfected this innovative tactic, and it changed warfare forever.

While Germany focused on its offensive capabilities, Britain and France took the opposite approach. The Allies dug in and focused on defense instead. They prepared for a repeat of the static fighting that was common in World War I. But General Heinz Guderian, one of the architects of blitzkrieg, recognized the weakness of the defensive strategy. He pioneered a more mobile and offensive approach to fighting, and he headed the German tank buildup in the late 1930s.

The success of blitzkrieg depended heavily on fast tanks that could strike quickly and effectively, catching the enemy by surprise. The tanks were concentrated into large formations that made up the spearhead of the attack. During World War I, tanks were used solely to support the infantry, or foot soldiers. However, the German panzer (tank) divisions of World War II were separate units. The panzers would strike at the heart of the enemy's defenses in aggressive attacks. The ultimate goal was to accomplish a quick and decisive victory with minimal losses. The mighty German air force also played an important role in blitzkrieg. The Luftwaffe bombed strategic targets and gained control of the airspace over the battlefield.

On September 1, 1939, Germany invaded Poland. For the first time, German blitzkrieg tactics were put into practice. At a time when the bulk of the German military still relied on horses and foot soldiers, attempting a blitzkrieg action in Poland was an enormous gamble. Tanks traveled at much higher speeds than the infantry, creating dangerous gaps in the lines. The infantry that followed behind had to march long distances to catch up to the armored units. Despite the risks, the campaign in Poland was swift. Although the Polish army fought hard, they were quickly overwhelmed by superior numbers and tactics. In less than a month, the entire nation had been overrun and occupied.

The Allies had severely underestimated the German war machine. Although Britain and France declared war on Germany after the invasion of Poland, subsequent military support never came, leaving the Polish army to fight alone. And although the Germans considered the Polish campaign a huge success, they suffered heavy losses and learned many lessons.

Throughout the winter of 1939–40, Germany rebuilt its army before turning its war machine to the west.

The Battle of France

From the outset of the campaign in the west, Hitler had his sights set on France. Historically, France was one of the world's strongest military powers, and its capital, Paris, was considered a prize to capture.

When the Germans prepared for an attack in the spring of 1940, the one thing that clearly stood in their way was the Maginot Line. The Maginot Line was a massive system of bunkers and weapon installations built by France in the 1930s along its border with Germany. It was designed to prevent German invasion and was considered to be a work of genius that was impossible to breach. Allied leaders felt that if a war was to come, it would be fought in the same way as in World War I. Battles would likely drag out for months, making a strong defensive line essential.

A GERMAN EQUESTRIAN PATROL ON THE AVENUE DE L'OPÉRA IN THE CAPITAL OF DEFEATED FRANCE, PARIS 1940

Protected to the north by the Maginot Line and to the south by the thick forests of the Ardennes region, which were considered too dense for tanks, France felt secure. Britain had even sent a 100,000-man expeditionary force to assist in fighting the inevitable German invasion. With this false sense of security, the French army prepared its defensive positions and awaited a German attack.

On May 10, blitzkrieg was put to the test like never before when Germany invaded France. Instead of going through the Maginot Line, the Germans simply went around it. The panzers rolled through the thick trees of the Ardennes in northern Luxembourg and southern Belgium—territory that the French had deemed impenetrable. This was a considerable risk, as the hilly terrain and dense foliage made operating tanks difficult. But within days it was clear that Germany had accomplished the impossible. Its forces quickly pushed their way through the Ardennes as the Luftwaffe soared overhead. The German planes had even succeeded in surprising the French air force on the ground, destroying dozens of aircraft before they even had a chance to take off.

The Germans efficiently forged their way through France, and on May 12, the Battle of Sedan began in the northeastern sector of the country. French and German forces faced off for two days in one of the most significant engagements in the larger Battle of France. They fought for control of the bridges over the river Meuse. German planes bombed French positions for several hours without pause, executing what would go down as the Luftwaffe's most intense bombardment of the entire war. Stuka dive-bombers, a fundamental element of blitzkrieg, made up a large part of the raid, dropping thousands of tons of explosives.

These attacks had a strong psychological effect on the French ground forces. It has been reported that the intense bombing caused French soldiers to abandon their positions even before the ground assault began. This German victory would mark a turning point in the war. The panzers easily crossed the Meuse, providing a direct route into the heart of France. By May 21, the first German tanks had reached the English Channel and effectively encircled 35 Allied divisions. The unbelievable speed and success of the German advance destroyed French morale. Britain and France were not only outfought; they were also outthought. France's military was among the largest in the world, and their tanks rivaled those of their German counterparts. But poor planning and leadership crushed any hopes of a French victory.

The Miracle at Dunkirk

By late May, Hitler's armies had pushed toward the northern coast of France, surrounding several hundred thousand Allied troops at the small port town of Dunkirk. With the

Germans closing in, it soon became clear that the Battle of France was lost. The British and French commanders were taken by surprise at the speed of the enemy advance, and more than 400,000 Allied troops were now surrounded, their backs to the North Sea. As the German forces encircled them, the cornered Allied troops established a perimeter and awaited their fate.

Across the English Channel, British prime minister Neville Chamberlain resigned under strong political pressure and was replaced by Winston Churchill. At first, Churchill and the British military leaders opposed evacuating Dunkirk. They believed that the Allied troops could hold out, but it soon became apparent that evacuation was the only option to save the trapped armies. On May 26, 1940, the British launched Operation Dynamo and began the evacuation of their troops. But Dunkirk's shallow beaches meant that large warships could pick up soldiers only from the town's sea wall, which extended into deep water. As a result, Dynamo got off to a slow start. Only 7,669 soldiers were evacuated on the first day, followed by just over 10,000 the next day. At that rate, the British would be able to save only a fraction of their force.

In a desperate attempt to speed up the evacuation, the British Royal Navy put out a call for all available small vessels to join in the effort. After assembling at the Strait of Dover, where the distance between England and France is just 21 miles, more than 800 boats crossed the English Channel to save their countrymen. The heroic fleet of fishing boats, sailboats, tugboats, barges, yachts, steamers, and even fireboats played an invaluable role in the rescue. From May 26 to June 4, 1940, an estimated 338,000 British and French troops were rescued. The massive operation became known as the "Miracle of Dunkirk." Unable to save their heavy equipment, the British were forced to leave behind the bulk of their tanks, machine guns, and artillery. In addition, some 80,000 British and French troops were left behind and captured by the Germans.

UP FOR DEBATE: THE FRENCH ARMY

Since the end of the war, many historians have debated the effectiveness of the French armed forces during World War II. It has been suggested in recent years that French soldiers were cowardly—that they fled in the face of the enemy and surrendered their country without firing a shot. But exactly how accurate are these claims? Although the French army was defeated quite rapidly during the Battle of France, their courage in defending their homeland and assisting their allies was apparent. At the evacuation of Dunkirk, many French soldiers stayed behind, guarding the rear. Without the French, there would have been no Miracle of Dunkirk, and the war could have easily taken a much different turn. But the French war effort didn't end in 1940. More than 500,000 Frenchmen joined the Allies in their fight across Europe, making a notable contribution to victory over Germany.

On June 22, 1940, France capitulated. German and French officers signed an armistice in the same train car where, 22 years earlier, the Germans had signed the armistice ending World War I. While the German blitzkrieg in France was undoubtedly successful and served as a humiliation for the French people, the evacuation of Dunkirk proved to be an equally critical moment. Hundreds of thousands of soldiers were spared to fight another day, providing a glimmer of hope for Great Britain. In a speech to the country, Churchill affirmed, "We shall fight on the beaches, we shall fight on the landing grounds, we shall fight in the fields and in the streets, we shall fight in the hills; we shall never surrender…" His now-iconic words inspired the people of Great Britain to carry on their war against Germany.

Hitler had hoped that the defeat at Dunkirk would lead Britain to negotiate an end to the conflict. Instead, the Miracle at Dunkirk rallied the nation in its fight against Germany. But for many of the rescued troops, Dunkirk was just the beginning of a long war. By the summer of 1940, Germany had defeated and occupied Poland, Denmark, Norway, Belgium, the Netherlands, Luxembourg, and France. Britain now stood alone against Hitler.

A MATTER OF CHOICE: EVACUATING THE BEACH

By late May 1940, German panzer divisions were prepared to deliver their final blow against the approximately 400,000 British and French troops trapped at Dunkirk. But on May 24 the panzers were ordered to halt, confusing many German field commanders. What caused such hesitation and who gave the command remains a mystery. However, it is clear that if the panzers had been allowed to continue, the encircled troops would have been driven into the sea. General Heinz Guderian, the German panzer commander in France, later said in his memoirs that the decision had "a most disastrous influence on the whole future course of the war."

The Submarine Threat: The Battle of the Atlantic

As war raged on land across the European continent, another key battle was taking place at sea. By the start of World War II, Nazi Germany had amassed one of the world's strongest fleets of submarines: the *Unterseeboots* ("undersea boats"), famously known as U-boats.

The Treaty of Versailles terms of 1918 had ordered Germany to surrender all of its submarines and cease all further production. But when Adolf Hitler rose to power, he promptly resumed submarine construction. When war broke out in 1939, Germany had only 57 U-boats. Yet, these undersea vessels found great success against a British navy that largely comprised massive battleships and other surface craft. The British ships were ineffective against the stealthy German submarines. Still, U-boats faced one major disadvantage in the early months of the war: Germany was not situated on the Atlantic Ocean. This meant that the German submarines had to travel long distances to reach British ships.

When the Germans occupied France and Norway in 1940, they instantly had access to ports that led directly into the Atlantic. The U-boats now had a shorter path to their targets, and they could conserve fuel and stay underwater longer. These advantages allowed them to start operating in "wolf packs," traveling in large groups to intercept and destroy convoys. For more than three years, German submarines ruled the Atlantic. The Allied warships defending the shipping convoys were overwhelmed. Before the occupation of France, U-boats sank roughly 80,000 tons of British ships; after July 1940, that number rose to nearly 230,000 tons per month. Allied warships could do little to prevent the devastating losses that occurred during the Battle of the Atlantic.

A BRITISH SHIP DEPLOYS A DEPTH CHARGE IN THE BATTLE OF
THE ATLANTIC, 1943

The German U-boat fleet relied heavily on an encryption device called the Enigma machine. This device allowed naval headquarters to secretly communicate with their boats. On the outside, Enigma machines looked like simple typewriters. But inside they contained a sophisticated system of rotating mechanisms that converted words into a code. The Germans considered these codes unbreakable; however, in July 1941, British cryptologists (code breakers) succeeded in breaking the Enigma code. The Allies were now able to read German messages and know when and where the U-boats were preparing to strike. This was the first significant step that led to the downfall of the U-boat menace. Still, breaking Enigma was not enough.

By March 1943, Germany had nearly succeeded in cutting off all supply routes from the United States to Great Britain. The United States had joined the conflict and was deep into the war alongside the Allies. In May, improvements in anti-submarine warfare began to significantly reduce the U-boat threat. Aircraft carriers and long-range reconnaissance aircraft, as well as destroyers and other escort vessels, were finally starting to master tactics to destroy U-boats. Radar was also introduced, enabling Allied warships to locate and track submerged enemy submarines. Combined with the intercepted Enigma transmissions, the Allies finally had the means to strike back. Within a few months, the Germans withdrew, effectively ending the Battle of the Atlantic.

Although the Allies and Germans were pitted against each other during the Battle of the Atlantic, honor among sailors was universal. Throughout World War II, Germany produced 1,162 U-boats. By the end of the war in 1945, 785 had been destroyed. And although the U-boats sank thousands of ships, they often showed mercy toward survivors. Amid the losses on both sides, there was a certain respect among "men of the sea."

ARMS AND ARMOR: THE TYPE VII U-BOAT

The Type VII U-boat is regarded as one of World War II's most influential weapons. The brilliantly designed submarine was fast, stealthy, and lethal. In its five years of service, Type VII U-boats sank nearly 3,000 ships, a total of 14.1 million tons, more than any other type of submarine in World War II. However, they also suffered the highest losses of any sub in the conflict. For this, they gained the nickname "iron coffins." More than 700 Type VII U-boats were built over the course of the war, making it the most produced submarine of all time. Today, just one survives.

The Battle of Britain

Following victory over France on June 22, 1940, Hitler set his sights on Great Britain, the last nation that stood against him in western Europe. The only way Germany could invade Britain was to cross the English Channel and land troops on the coast. German military leaders organized a massive invasion. Its code name was Operation Sea Lion. Large concentrations of troops and equipment were staged in France, poised to cross the Channel. While Britain's forces had been severely weakened, they still had the mighty Royal Air Force (RAF). For Operation Sea Lion to succeed, the Germans needed air superiority over the Channel, which could only be accomplished by eliminating the RAF from the skies.

By the start of World War II in 1939, the Luftwaffe was the most powerful air force in the world. The Luftwaffe was led by World War I fighter pilot ace Hermann Göring. He assured Hitler that he could effortlessly destroy the RAF within a matter of days and secure safe passage for the invasion. In July 1940, the Battle of Britain began as the RAF and Luftwaffe faced off in the skies. But, unlike in previous campaigns, the Luftwaffe was now facing a first-class opponent. Most German pilots flew the Messerschmitt Bf 109. This fighter plane was arguably the best in the world at the time. Meanwhile, the British took to the controls of the Hawker Hurricane and Supermarine Spitfire. The Spitfire was well-liked among pilots. It soon became a symbol of the Battle of Britain and defiance against the German onslaught.

Although Britain was fighting alone against Germany in 1940, nearly a quarter of the RAF pilots came from other countries, including Poland, New Zealand, Australia, Czechoslovakia, Canada, Belgium, France, South Africa, and even the United States. These foreign volunteers proved to be invaluable in the desperate fight to control the skies. One of Britain's most valuable assets was radar, known as "radio direction finding," or RDF. RDF was a means of learning what direction enemy planes were coming from in order to prepare for them. A chain of 29 radio direction finding stations along the coast allowed the RAF to detect German aircraft up to 100 miles away. This gave fighter squadrons ample time to scramble their aircraft and intercept the enemy.

By the end of October 1940, after more than three months of aerial combat, the British emerged victorious. Hitler was forced to admit defeat and cancel Operation Sea Lion.

Success in the Battle of Britain had a significant immediate effect as well as a long-term impact on the outcome of the war. The resilience of the British military, and in particular the RAF, allowed Great Britain to remain free from Nazi occupation. The Battle of Britain was the first military engagement in history to be fought almost exclusively in the air and marked Germany's first major defeat in World War II. For the British, it was the start of a long and difficult road to victory.

The Blitz

As the Battle of Britain drew to a close in September 1940, a dark new period in the history of the British Isles was just beginning. When Germany failed to defeat the RAF, the Luftwaffe shifted tactics. German planes started bombing civilian targets in an effort to crush the morale of the British people and strike terror in the heart of the country.

On September 7, 1940, German planes raided London. This was the first of countless nights of bombing that would come to be known as the "Blitz." While London was the main target, the British cities of Birmingham, Liverpool, Coventry, and Glasgow were also bombed. Daily attacks destroyed thousands

A GERMAN AIR RAID OVER CENTRAL LONDON, 1940

of homes and businesses, annihilated communities, and tore apart families. The civilian casualties were massive. Children were evacuated to the countryside, and strict rationing was ongoing due to food shortages caused by U-Boats sinking supply ships.

As German aircraft approached, people were warned by loud sirens and led to underground shelters by air raid wardens. Communal shelters, including train tunnels, were widely used, while individual shelters in private homes were also common. Air raid wardens risked their lives during and after bombing raids, rescuing people trapped in the rubble, putting out fires, and providing medical care to wounded civilians.

Although casualties were high, the attacks had little effect on Britain's war effort. In fact, the resilience shown by the British people left a profound impression on foreigners, especially American journalist Edward R. Murrow. His frequent radio broadcasts from London revealed to the world—and, most importantly, to America—that Britain would endure against Nazi Germany. While the United States was not yet ready to enter the war, President Franklin Roosevelt pledged his full support to the British. This powerful statement was backed up with military support in the form of aircraft, tanks, and ammunition.

By May 1941, Hitler realized that he would be unable to force the British into submission. Instead, he shifted his attention to eastern Europe. On May 10, 1941, the Luftwaffe raided London for the last time, killing 1,364 people and wounding more than 1,600. It marked the highest number of casualties of any raid on the United Kingdom. The Blitz lasted over eight months, and more than 43,000 people lost their lives. It was a time of great suffering for the British people. Nonetheless, the country remained vigilant and intact amid the destruction. As Britain began rebuilding its cities, another chapter of World War II was about to unfold, with Hitler turning to his next target: the Soviet Union.

CHAPTER 3

GERMANY MOVES EAST

The Eastern Front saw some of World War II's most brutal fighting. The invasion of the Soviet Union began much like Germany's earlier campaigns. After a string of quick victories, the Wehrmacht, Germany's armed forces, approached the gates of Moscow. But unlike Hitler's previous attacks, the tide was turning. A long and devastating war was about to begin. Millions would suffer on an unprecedented scale in a campaign that would change the history of warfare forever.

★ ★ ★

Operation Barbarossa

After conquering nearly every nation in western Europe, Adolf Hitler set his sights on a new target: the Union of Soviet Socialist Republics (USSR). The Soviet Union was a communist nation formed after World War I by means of a violent revolution in the former Russian Empire. During World War II, the USSR was led by Joseph Stalin, a brutal dictator who ruled with an iron fist. Although Hitler and Stalin stood on opposite ends of the political spectrum, both were totalitarian leaders with little regard for human rights. One of the most notable differences between the two was their ideology. Hitler preached that Germans were a "master race," destined to rule all others. Stalin's brutality, on the other hand, was in support of communist ideology rather than racial intolerance. Still, both dictators sought to expand their rule at the expense of others.

Surprise Attack

Conquering the Soviet Union and repopulating it with Germans was one of Hitler's earliest ambitions. But with the Molotov-Ribbentrop nonaggression pact between the two nations still in effect in 1941, Stalin did not believe that Germany would attack. He was unaware that Hitler always considered the agreement to be a temporary measure. By mid-1941, Germany had the strongest and most feared military in the world. After a string of successful campaigns across Europe, the Wehrmacht had become an experienced and highly disciplined fighting force. Large concentrations of German troops were now assembled at the Soviet border, while the Luftwaffe repeatedly flew deep into Soviet airspace, testing their capabilities. Still, Stalin ignored the indications of war.

GERMAN TROOPS CROSSING THE SOVIET BORDER DURING OPERATION BARBAROSSA

On June 22, 1941, Nazi Germany launched Operation Barbarossa, a surprise attack against the Soviet Union. In one of the largest military operations in modern history, more than three million soldiers and 3,000 tanks smashed into the heart of Soviet territory. The German army attacked along a line stretching 2,000 miles, from the Baltic Sea in the north to the Black Sea in the south, overwhelming anyone, soldiers or civilians, in their path and taking hundreds of thousands of prisoners. In the first month of the invasion, German forces encircled large concentrations of troops in the cities of Minsk and Smolensk while panzer tanks rolled toward Moscow and Leningrad. Hitler anticipated a quick and decisive victory over the Soviets in just a few weeks. Everything was going almost too well.

Unlike the campaigns in the west, the war in the east was waged with unimaginable ruthlessness. The Germans marched into the USSR as conquerors determined to enslave the Slavic peoples and exterminate the nation's sizable Jewish population. Millions of Soviet prisoners of war and civilians were killed. Mobile death squads, known as *Einsatzgruppen,* began the mass murder of Soviet Jews.

The Soviets Strike Back

But after the success of the blitzkrieg in the early weeks of Operation Barbarossa, the Germans underestimated how far the Soviet people would go to defend themselves. As the Germans advanced, they found nothing but burning buildings, evidence of the Soviet "scorched earth" policy. As primitive as it seems, this practice achieved great success in denying the Germans much-needed resources. In addition, the Soviets could afford to sacrifice both soldiers and territory, because they had plenty of both. When planning the invasion, the Germans wrongly calculated that on top of the 150 currently active Soviet divisions, only an additional 50 could be recruited. By the middle of August, just one month after the start of Operation Barbarossa, the Soviets had formed more than 200 new divisions, for a total of 360. Consequently, as the Germans pushed onward, they soon found their path blocked. German supplies started to run short. Although the road to victory for Hitler's armies seemed to be open, it was clear the campaign wouldn't be as quick as anticipated.

The Battle of Moscow

In early October 1941, the Germans launched Operation Typhoon, sending a massive force to seize Moscow, the Soviet capital. The German high command planned to capture the city in a swift drive before winter. Led by blitzkrieg tactician General Heinz Guderian, the advance quickly overpowered the weak and retreating Soviet forces. The Germans captured the strategic towns of Kaluga and Mozhaisk, the latter only about 70 miles from Moscow. With the German threat looming, the citizens of Moscow prepared to defend their city. Men and women of all ages were conscripted to build three lines of fortifications and surrounding defenses. Anti-tank obstacles and barriers were erected in the streets, and the military placed artillery and machine guns in strategic positions. Large numbers of troops were brought in from Siberia and other faraway regions.

By October 15, Guderian's army was within striking distance of the capital, just 18 miles from the city center. But when the Germans reached the gates of Moscow, the strong and determined Russian resistance held out. As the Wehrmacht prepared to make their final assault, heavy rains turned roads into swamps, bogging down tanks and troops. In November, when the temperature dropped and the mud froze, the Germans resumed their offensive. But with the onset of winter, they now faced an even greater threat.

A Long, Cold Winter

The winter of 1941–42 was unusually harsh, even by Russian standards. Temperatures plunged to minus 40 degrees Fahrenheit, freezing German tanks and weapons. Guderian's blitzkrieg came to a sudden halt. In their confidence that the battle would be over before winter, the Germans failed to issue their troops any winter provisions. Lacking gloves, boots, coats, and other necessary gear to survive a winter campaign, thousands of German soldiers froze to death. As the situation grew increasingly dire, Hitler was forced to halt the drive with victory literally in sight: There were reports that German soldiers could see the spires of the Kremlin, a fortified palace where Stalin resided, through their binoculars. Guderian's army was forced to make a slow and costly retreat.

In December 1942, motivated by their success in halting the German onslaught on Moscow, the Soviet army counterattacked. The Red Army advanced nearly 200 miles into German-occupied territory. But by late January, the Soviet counteroffensive had lost its momentum. The two foes were in a bitter stalemate that lasted until the spring of 1943. Both sides dug in and struggled to survive amid the freezing temperatures. While the campaign in Russia would continue for years, the Soviets proved that the German army was not invincible. With a little help from the infamous Russian winter, the Soviets had prevented the fall of their capital and stopped the blitzkrieg dead in its tracks. The war against the Soviet Union would drain Germany's manpower and resources for the remainder of the conflict.

The Siege of Leningrad

In September 1941, German artillery began shelling Leningrad (now called Saint Petersburg), the former capital of the Russian Empire and one of the Soviet Union's largest cities. Named after Vladimir Lenin, the founder of the Communist Party and leader of the Russian Revolution, Leningrad was a target of great symbolic importance. Although it was not tactically important to the German war effort, the city represented the Soviet regime and was, therefore, a principal ideological target in Hitler's crusade against communism. Soviet general Georgy

Zhukov was sent to Leningrad shortly after the Germans began their bombardment. His task was to transform the city into an impenetrable fortress. Hundreds of thousands of civilians erected defenses in and around the city. After several weeks of fortifying, the Soviets waited and anticipated a full-on assault on Leningrad. But it never came.

Adolf Hitler had initially planned to capture the city and burn it to the ground. But as German troops awaited the order to begin the assault, Hitler changed his mind. Rather than suffer the heavy losses of a long battle, he proposed a siege that would cut Leningrad off from the world. Hitler also realized that if Germany occupied the city, they would be forced to feed its enormous population. The Wehrmacht was already struggling to feed its millions of soldiers fighting in Russia and couldn't afford to provide food for millions of Soviet civilians as well.

A Winter of Starvation

Instead of an attack, the German troops besieged Leningrad. Their aim was to let the population wither away due to mass starvation. By late September 1941, Leningrad was almost entirely encircled. Failure to evacuate the city's population became one of the Soviet regime's biggest blunders of the war. Two and a half million civilians, including 400,000 children, were trapped in Leningrad.

With the last roads to the outside blocked, severe hunger began to set in. Rationing had already been instituted before the siege started, but with access to supplies now eliminated, daily rations became three times smaller. Working citizens were allotted 250 grams (8.8 ounces) of bread per day, while the majority of the population was allowed just 125 grams (4.4 ounces, or just over five slices). Loaves of bread consisted mainly of sawdust due to the scarcity of flour. Meat was virtually nonexistent, and dogs, cats, birds, and other animals disappeared from the streets, eaten in desperation by the starving citizens of Leningrad. An average meal consisted of wallpaper and soup made of boiled leather, a diet that led to widespread malnutrition and illness. Unsurprisingly, within the first month of the siege, several cases of cannibalism were recorded, a number that would grow into the thousands as months went on. The starved population lived in freezing apartments alongside their dead. As firewood ran out, furniture, floorboards, and eventually books were burned to generate heat.

Hitler was determined to wipe Leningrad off the map. The Germans continued to bomb the city relentlessly, adding to the suffering. In the winter of 1942, the city's water pipes froze and broke, depriving the residents of drinking water. Death rates spiked, and corpses littered the once lively streets. Efforts were made to resupply the city via Lake Ladoga. When the lake froze over, an ice road become operational. Known as the "Road of Life," the legendary route became the lifeline of Leningrad. Hundreds of trucks crossed the dangerous road every day, delivering supplies and evacuating refugees. But driving across thin ice, and under constant aerial attack from the Luftwaffe, few trucks got through. Many supplies—and civilians—went to the bottom of the icy lake. Still, the heroism and resilience displayed by the drivers who risked their lives became a symbol of hope.

The siege did not end until January 27, 1944, some 872 days after it began. It is estimated that between 1.6 million and 2 million people perished between 1941 and 1944. Most died of starvation or hypothermia. It was the largest loss of life ever known in a modern city. Some historians refer to the siege as a racially motivated genocide, characteristic of the German war of extermination against the Soviet Union. The tragedy that was Leningrad remains one of the worst humanitarian disasters in history.

The Second Battle of Kharkov

In October 1941, the German blitzkrieg advanced across the Soviet Union and captured Kharkov, a city located in present-day Ukraine. It was a relatively quick battle for German forces. (It is now known as the First Battle of Kharkov.) The Wehrmacht continued its drive deeper into Russia, fighting toward Moscow, its primary objective. A year later, in May 1942, Soviet forces succeeded in defending their capital and were now determined to retake territory lost to the German blitzkrieg of 1941. After their counteroffensive following the German failure to capture Moscow, the Red Army secured a large bulge in the front lines and came within striking distance of Kharkov.

On the morning of May 12, a massive artillery and aerial bombardment of the German lines marked the start of the Second Battle of Kharkov. Despite the intensity and accuracy of these strikes, they had little effect on the German forces defending the city. Most soldiers were trained to survive heavy bombing. Two hours later, once the shelling and air attacks ceased, Soviet Marshal Semyon Timoshenko launched a ground assault to retake the city. The attack had a promising start as Red Army forces penetrated several miles through German defenses. Mass panic ensued among the German troops as they realized they were being overrun. Numerous soldiers fled their positions, enabling the Soviets to push forward with minimal opposition. The German ground forces quickly regrouped, however, while the Luftwaffe took to the skies in large numbers. Fighter planes patrolled above the battlefield, destroying numerous Soviet planes in the air and on the ground.

As the second day of fighting unfolded on May 13, German forces gradually pushed the Soviets back, bolstered by a strong force of bombers that flew overhead. By May 17, the Germans had organized an attack. Their goal was to surround the attacking Red Army. Over the next several days of heavy fighting, the Germans continued to push the Soviets back. On May 22, the Germans ultimately succeeded in cutting off Marshal Timoshenko's army from the rest of the Soviet forces. The 250,000 men trapped inside the pocket were subjected to murderous artillery and machine-gun fire as well as a massive aerial bombardment. Finally, on May 28, 1942, after six days of encirclement, the Soviet forces surrendered.

Much of the failure in the battle can be attributed to poor planning by Red Army officers and Joseph Stalin. The Soviets had greatly underestimated the strength of German defenses at Kharkov and overestimated the capabilities of their attacking force. Their inability to recapture the city—and the surrender of nearly a quarter of a million fighting soldiers—was a serious setback for the Soviets. For the moment, it seemed that Hitler's armies still had the upper hand on the Eastern Front.

The Battle of Stalingrad

Since the beginning of the campaign in Russia, Hitler was fixed on the idea of taking the industrial city of Stalingrad, named after his archenemy. Located on the western bank of the Volga River, Stalingrad would see some of World War II's most brutal fighting. As determined as the Germans were to capture it, the Soviets were just as determined to hold it. In the summer of 1942, as the Germans advanced on Stalingrad, the city prepared its defenses. Nearly all of the young men had gone to fight, so women and children got to work digging trenches and building fortifications to defend their city.

RED ARMY SOLDIERS IN THE RUINS OF STALINGRAD, 1942–43

On August 23, 1942, the Germans began their assault. The battle started with massive bombing, reducing the city to a smoldering ruin. Nearly every building was bombed or set ablaze, and a thick layer of ash blanketed what remained. The Soviets defended Stalingrad street by street, house by house, and room by room. There were times where the Germans occupied the bottom floor of a building while the Soviets held the floor above. The destroyed buildings were also ideal for snipers, which both sides utilized in great numbers. A maze of tunnels and trenches ran across the city, serving as fighting positions for both German and Soviet troops. The nonstop combat was incredibly straining for both sides, but the Germans slowly gained the upper hand as they poured hundreds of thousands of well-trained soldiers into the offensive.

By mid-October 1942, the Germans were close to victory. Stalingrad's Soviet defenders had managed to hold part of the city's northern factory district, which served as their final defensive line. When Lieutenant General Vasily Chuikov, commander of Soviet forces in Stalingrad, was asked how he planned to hold the city, he replied, "We will defend the city or die in the attempt." Reinforcements were ferried across the Volga in large numbers, constantly under heavy attack. The casualties were staggering, but the troops that did make it across played a major role in gaining a foothold on the riverbank and keeping at least some of the ruined city in Soviet hands.

The onset of winter again caused problems for both sides. The freezing temperatures made tanks and weapons difficult to operate and proved deadly to the frontline soldiers. The Germans were ill-equipped for cold weather and suffered greatly in the winter of 1942–43. The Red Army had better clothing for winter warfare, including quilted jackets known as *telogreikas* and fur hats called *ushankas*. Soviet casualties were extremely high, but the Battle of Stalingrad also caused tremendous losses and numerous logistical problems for the Germans. Hitler had fired several of his top generals over their failure to take Stalingrad and was now making many command decisions himself. His frantic desire to seize the city led to many irrational and poor tactical decisions. These mistakes severely affected the entire Russian front. With the fighting inside the city taking a heavy toll, Hitler pulled units from abroad to replace the ones that were decimated. Other Axis troops sent to the city, including Italians and Romanians, were poorly trained and had low morale. They became the first targets of the massive Soviet counterattack in November of 1942. Within three days of the attack, Soviet forces led by General Georgy Zhukov had surrounded the city, turning the tide of the battle.

General Friedrich Paulus, commander of German forces in the city, asked Hitler for permission to break out of the encirclement. Paulus was confident that he could save his ensnared army, but Hitler refused. Instead, Hitler promised to resupply the troops by air and ordered them to hold their ground at all costs. The air resupply operation was a catastrophe. It cost the Luftwaffe hundreds of aircraft and managed to deliver only a fraction of the promised supplies. Without enough fuel, food, and ammunition, the Germans could no longer wage war against the superior Soviet force. By February 2, 1943, the last German troops in Stalingrad surrendered, although scattered fighting in the city continued until March.

A MATTER OF CHOICE: THE DECISION AT STALINGRAD

In the winter of 1942, when German forces were trapped in Stalingrad, Hitler ordered them to hold their positions. German general Friedrich Paulus believed that he could break his army out, but Hitler was obsessed with taking the city. If Paulus had been allowed to attempt a breakout and retreat, much of the German force may have been spared to fight another day. Hitler's fateful indecision at Stalingrad was one of the main factors that led to the collapse of the Wehrmacht on the Eastern Front.

Stalingrad was one of the bloodiest battles in human history. More than 850,000 Axis soldiers were killed, wounded, or captured, while Soviet casualties numbered close to a million. In addition, more than 40,000 men, women, and children perished—nearly the entire civilian population. The defeat was crushing to Nazi Germany, and the losses to the Wehrmacht would prove fatal to the German war effort. In Russia today, the Battle of Stalingrad is remembered as one of the most famous battles of "the Great Patriotic War." While the price paid for victory was high, its impact on the war was immeasurable, making it one of the most celebrated achievements of the Soviet Union in World War II.

The Battle of Kursk

By the summer of 1943, German forces in Russia were still struggling to recover from the crushing defeat at Stalingrad. In July, Hitler launched Operation Citadel, attempting to resume the Wehrmacht's offensive in the Soviet Union. The operation focused on a large body of Soviet forces located inside a 150-mile bulge in the front lines near the city of Kursk in western Russia. Also known as a salient, the bulge held over a million Soviet soldiers and a large number of tanks and artillery. The Germans hoped to surround and destroy this force. In preparation for the battle, roughly one-third of Germany's entire military strength was staged near Kursk. The force included 900,000 soldiers, 10,000 artillery pieces, 2,700 tanks, and 2,000 aircraft. Soviet soldiers inside the salient numbered close to 1.3 million and were supported by 20,000 artillery pieces, 3,600 tanks, and 2,400 aircraft. With vast numbers of troops and equipment at the ready, the stage was set for the monumental battle that followed.

On the morning of July 5, 1943, the clash between German and Soviet forces commenced. Initially, the Germans were able to surpass the Soviet frontline defenses. They advanced 10 miles into the salient from the north and 30 miles from the south. Regardless of the territorial gains, the operation resulted in heavy German tank losses. On July 12, after several days of widespread fighting, the Battle of Kursk reached its climax at the village of Prokhorovka. Nearly 2,000 tanks engaged in the largest tank battle in history. The mass-produced Soviet T-34 tank faced off against the elite German Tiger tank, a matchup that heavily favored the Germans. But despite the Nazi advantage, the Soviets swiftly gained the upper hand and launched a successful counterattack. Most importantly, German Enigma messages decoded by British intelligence helped turn the tide of the battle. The

GERMAN PANZER III TANKS AT THE BATTLE OF KURSK, SOVIET UNION, 1943

advance warning gave the Soviets details of the German assault. Russian aircraft, along with minefields and anti-tank obstacles, also played a significant role in halting the German advance. By July 14, Hitler's troops were forced to retreat from Prokhorovka.

The successful counterattack at Kursk evolved into a powerful offensive that led the Red Army to recapture several German-held cities by mid-August. The Battle of Kursk marked the last German blitzkrieg in Russia. The battle lasted five and a half weeks and sealed the fate of the Wehrmacht in the east, forcing it to retreat on all fronts. More than 200,000 German soldiers were killed, wounded, or went missing at Kursk. The losses in tanks and other armored vehicles numbered into the thousands. The Soviets now had the upper hand on the Eastern Front. They were determined to liberate their country and push the fascists back to Berlin.

UP FOR DEBATE: THE LARGEST TANK BATTLE

The Battle of Kursk was a turning point of the war on the Eastern Front. It is widely recognized as the largest tank battle of all time. Since the war, some historians have debated the accuracy of these claims, pointing out that the Battle of Brody two years earlier was in fact a larger tank battle. On June 23, 1941, the day after the start of Operation Barbarossa, the Germans and Soviets engaged in a massive tank battle near Brody, Poland. While the exact numbers are unknown, some sources estimate that 1,000 German panzers and 3,000 Soviet tanks were present. The Battle of Kursk is better documented and publicized, partly due to the fact that it was a Soviet victory, while Brody resulted in defeat. To this day, opinions remain sharply divided with regard to the sizes of the two decisive tank battles.

CHAPTER 4

THE PACIFIC THEATER

On December 7, 1941, America was compelled to enter World War II. The United States joined the Allied Powers of Great Britain, Free France, and the Soviet Union. The new front for the conflict became known as the Pacific theater. Four long years of combat on land, in the air, and on the sea would result in the destruction of the Japanese Empire and the emergence of the United States as the world's strongest military power.

Pearl Harbor

When the Japanese invaded China in 1937, the United States responded with a host of economic sanctions and trade embargoes. As a small island nation, Japan relied heavily on trade, making these restrictions crippling. American officials believed that these constraints, especially the oil embargo, would force Japan to halt its conquests across Asia. But despite the devastating setbacks, the Japanese Empire continued to expand. Despite the fact that tensions between the two nations ran high, no one believed that the Japanese would launch an attack on American soil.

Although Hawaii did not become a state until 1959, the territory was home to one of America's most important naval bases: Pearl Harbor. In 1940, as a response to the growing hostility between the United States and Japan, the U.S. Navy moved its massive Pacific Fleet to Pearl Harbor to take up a strong position. Located about 2,500 miles from the U.S. mainland, naval leaders felt that Pearl Harbor would protect American interests in the Pacific and deter further Japanese aggression. They believed that if the Japanese were to attack, they would focus on one of the European colonies in the South Pacific: the Dutch East Indies (now Indonesia), the British-held island of Singapore, or French Indochina (present-day Vietnam, Laos, and Cambodia). Because American military leaders did not expect an attack so close to home, Pearl Harbor was left relatively unprotected. Almost the entire Pacific Fleet was docked around Ford Island, while hundreds of airplanes were stored in tight formations on nearby airfields. Fearing potential sabotage from the large Japanese-American population living in Hawaii, the aircraft were clustered together, away from fences and roads. It would be challenging to sabotage the planes from the ground but simple to destroy all of them at once from the air.

In early 1941, Admiral Isoroku Yamamoto was appointed commander in chief of the Imperial Japanese Navy's Combined Fleet. Almost immediately, he began planning to eliminate the greatest threat that stood in the way of Japanese expansion in the Pacific. He developed a daring and sophisticated plan to launch a surprise carrier-based air attack on Pearl Harbor. The aim was to destroy the Pacific Fleet and give the Japanese forces free rein in Asia. In late November 1941, the Japanese began a series of peace negotiations with the American government. This clever distraction allowed the Japanese time to secretly prepare their aircraft carriers for war. On November 26, Vice Admiral Chuichi Nagumo left from Japan in command of six aircraft carriers—the *Akagi*, the *Kaga*, the *Soryu*, the *Hiryu*, the *Shokaku*, and the *Zuikaku*. Supported by an armada of battleships, destroyers, cruisers, and submarines, Nagumo steamed toward Pearl Harbor. Maintaining strict radio silence and avoiding regular ocean routes, the Japanese strike force succeeded in remaining undetected as they headed to a rendezvous point about 1,000 miles north of Hawaii.

On the morning of December 7, 1941, the Japanese launched their attack. Hundreds of fighter planes took off from the decks of the six aircraft carriers. The Americans were completely surprised when the first aircraft began bombing Pearl Harbor at approximately 7:48 a.m. local time. Many sailors were still asleep and caught completely off guard. Japanese planes filled the sky, dropping their bombs among the clustered U.S. Navy warships and strafing (repeatedly attacking with bombs or machine-gun fire from low-flying aircraft) the panicked soldiers and sailors onshore. One of the most tragic disasters of the attack was the battleship USS *Arizona*, which was struck by a 1,760-pound bomb, triggering a massive explosion. The 33,000-ton vessel was launched out of the water, killing 1,177 sailors and marines almost instantly.

IN ADDITION TO THE USS *ARIZONA*, THE USS *WEST VIRGINIA*, SHOWN HERE, WAS BURNED AFTER THE ATTACK AT PEARL HARBOR, HAWAII, 1941

The surprise attack damaged or destroyed 21 American ships and more than 300 aircraft. Of the casualties, 2,403 men, women, and children died, and another 1,100 were wounded. Following the attack on Pearl Harbor, the Japanese made simultaneous strikes on the U.S. territories of the Philippines, Guam, and Wake Island, as well as the British colonies of Malaya, Hong Kong, and Singapore. Despite the incredible losses and the shockwaves that the Pearl Harbor attack sent across the world, the Japanese ultimately failed to destroy the entire Pacific Fleet. All of the U.S. Navy's aircraft carriers were away from the base at the time, and most of Pearl Harbor's shipyards, submarine docks, and oil storage depots remained intact. But the damage had been done. Americans were bound and determined to "remember Pearl Harbor" and avenge those who gave their lives on December 7, 1941.

The day after the attack, President Franklin D. Roosevelt addressed Congress to ask for a declaration of war. His compelling speech would inspire the nation in its darkest hour. He opened with the following words: "Yesterday, December 7, 1941, a date which will live in infamy, the United States of America was suddenly and deliberately attacked by naval and air forces of the Empire of Japan." Roosevelt's words were followed by a near-unanimous vote that plunged the United States into the war. Following the U.S. declaration, Japan's allies, Germany and Italy, declared war on the United States. Although Japan had shocked the world with its surprise attack, Admiral Yamamoto knew that America would strike back with a vengeance. He famously stated, "I fear all we have done is to awaken a sleeping giant and fill him with a terrible resolve."

A MATTER OF CHOICE: AN ATTACK CALLED OFF

Admiral Isoroku Yamamoto's plan to destroy the U.S. Pacific Fleet was put into motion with the December 7, 1941, attack on Pearl Harbor, Hawaii. Two powerful waves of fighters inflicted a devastating surprise attack. More than 2,300 U.S. service members were killed, and the U.S. Navy and air forces stationed at Pearl Harbor were crippled. Despite the undeniable damage, the Japanese failed to completely destroy the fleet as Yamamoto had intended. With fuel running low and casualties beginning to set in, the Japanese chose not to launch a third wave of fighters. This left the American fuel reserves, repair docks, and other vital establishments untouched. If a third wave had attacked while American defenses were in turmoil, it could have resulted in further damage. Today, the failure to unleash a final wave of fighters on Pearl Harbor is seen as an enormous blunder for the Japanese and a stroke of luck for the battered U.S. Navy.

The Battle of the Coral Sea

The Japanese followed their Pearl Harbor attack with a string of victories across the Pacific, attacking and occupying American, British, and Dutch territories. In April of 1942, Japan made plans for an invasion of New Guinea, a crucial supply point for the Allies. New Guinea was the last defense that stood in the way of a Japanese invasion of Australia. To carry out their attack, the Japanese sought control of the Coral Sea in order to make an amphibious landing at Port Moresby in southeast New Guinea. But Allied code breakers intercepted Japan's plans, and a powerful fleet was sent to find the Japanese. On May 4, after several days of searching and minor skirmishes, the two armadas converged. This marked the start of the Battle of the Coral Sea. Each side possessed two aircraft carriers supported by a substantial fleet of warships. Under the command of Rear Admiral Frank J. Fletcher, the American force sailed in tight formation. Meanwhile, the Japanese commander, Rear Admiral Koso Abe, divided his fleet into several scattered groups. The Battle of the Coral Sea was the first naval engagement in history in which the ships of the opposing sides never saw each other; the entire battle was fought by carrier-based aircraft. Neither side had mastered this style of warfare yet, leading to numerous mistakes and valuable lessons for future campaigns.

In the opening stages of the battle, the inexperienced aviators frequently missed their targets or ran out of ammunition before reaching them. On May 7, three days into the engagement, the Americans gained the upper hand, sinking the Japanese aircraft carrier *Shoho*. The following day, a successful attack severely damaged the *Shokaku*, the second Japanese carrier. On May 8, the Imperial Japanese Navy launched a counterattack and severely damaged the American aircraft carriers USS *Yorktown* and USS *Lexington*. The *Lexington* was left crippled, and her surviving aircraft and crew were evacuated. The ship was later scuttled (deliberately sunk) to keep it from falling into enemy hands. Although both sides suffered equally heavy losses, the battle was a decisive strategic victory for the Allies. Facing substantial losses in aircraft, the Japanese were forced to postpone their invasion of New Guinea, marking the first time the Allies successfully stopped a Japanese advance. By May 8, both the Americans and the Japanese withdrew from the Coral Sea, saving their remaining ships to fight another day.

The battle was a historic event in naval history and marked the first of several major sea battles across the Pacific. Often called the battle that saved Australia, the Battle of the Coral Sea is commemorated every year by Australians. It undoubtedly prevented an imminent Japanese invasion of their country. The Battle of the Coral Sea left Japan's naval strength weakened, which had a significant impact on the outcome of the Battle of Midway a month later. The carrier *Shokaku* was so badly damaged that it was unable to be repaired in time, evening the odds for the underdog American fleet.

The Battle of Midway

After Japan's failure to fully destroy the U.S. Pacific Fleet at Pearl Harbor, and the enduring Japanese defeat in the Coral Sea, the powerful Imperial Japanese Navy turned toward Midway Island. Midway was a 2.4-square-mile atoll (a ring-shaped island enclosing a lagoon) that was home to one of the United States' most important military installations in the Pacific. If captured, the Japanese could use Midway as an air and sea base to make a second attack on Pearl Harbor and assert their dominance in the region.

By early 1942, U.S. Navy cryptologists had succeeded in breaking Japanese communication codes and could intercept and interpret most messages. This gave the Americans a clear advantage in the Pacific. In May, decoded messages gave the Navy advance warning that the Japanese were planning an attack at a new location somewhere in the Pacific. Intercepted messages referred to the target as "AF," code for an unspecified place. Navy cryptologists developed a brilliant ruse to reveal the location. The American base at Midway Island sent out a false, uncoded message stating that they were short of fresh water. Navy code breakers soon intercepted a Japanese communication that said that "AF" was short of fresh water. This confirmed that the target of their new attack was the essential U.S. base at Midway. Further decoded messages gave the Navy an estimated date for when the Japanese would strike and provided details of their plan. U.S. carrier forces were then sent to the east of the island and prepared to defend it at all costs.

US NAVY TORPEDO BOMBERS ABOARD THE USS *ENTERPRISE*, BATTLE OF MIDWAY, JUNE 1942

On the morning of June 4, 1942, Japanese carrier-based aircraft attacked Midway. The first wave of fighters severely damaged the base. Meanwhile, the main Japanese invasion force steamed on, unaware that the U.S. Navy was waiting for them. The Japanese force consisted of four aircraft carriers, seven battleships, nearly 150 support ships, 300 aircraft, and 15 submarines. Despite their advance knowledge of the attack, the Americans were outnumbered two to one. Just six months after the crippling attack at Pearl Harbor, the U.S. Navy was struggling to recover and muster a force powerful enough to challenge their enemy.

After their first strikes, the Japanese aircraft returned to their carriers to rearm and refuel. Only then did the Japanese become aware of the U.S. forces that were lurking nearby. American TBD Devastator torpedo bombers and SBD Dauntless dive-bombers took off from USS *Enterprise*, USS *Hornet*, and USS *Yorktown*. (The planes were manufactured by the Douglas Aircraft Company. The acronym *TBD* stands for *torpedo bomber Douglas*; *SBD* stands for *scout bomber Douglas*.) A fierce battle was soon underway. American aviators braved murderous antiaircraft fire to bomb the Japanese ships. Three of Japan's four aircraft carriers—the *Akagi*, the *Kaga*, and the *Soryu*—were put out of action, while the final carrier, the *Hiryu*, launched two air attacks against the American fleet. The USS *Yorktown* was severely damaged as a result. Later that afternoon, the *Hiryu* was sunk with all of its aircraft onboard, effectively eliminating the threat on Midway.

Over the next two days, the American forces continued their onslaught. The Japanese ultimately were forced to abandon the battle and retreat. Four aircraft carriers, one cruiser, and hundreds of aircraft—once the pride of Japan's mighty navy—now lay at the bottom of the ocean. More than 3,000 Japanese soldiers and sailors lost their lives. The United States lost approximately 360 men, one aircraft carrier (USS *Yorktown*), one destroyer (USS *Hammann*), and 144 aircraft.

Midway was a monumental military and propaganda victory for the United States, as the four Japanese carriers that had been sunk were all part of the fleet that facilitated the attack on Pearl Harbor. The victory at Midway stopped Japanese expansionism in its tracks and enabled the Americans to launch a series of invasions to defeat the now shrinking empire of Japan.

Guadalcanal

By 1942, Japan held territory in China, India, and on islands throughout the region, including American, British, and Dutch colonies. The Japanese Empire had expanded for years without any serious international intervention or repercussions. As a result, Japan developed a strong foothold that would prove tough to breach. But the prewar appeasement of Japan ended after Pearl Harbor. The United States was now bound and determined to bring an end to the Japanese regime and liberate its territorial conquests. While the war in Europe was of undeniable importance, the Pacific war was far more personal for most Americans. It was the Japanese who had struck U.S. territory and killed more than 2,400 American citizens. The war in the Pacific began at Pearl Harbor, on an island that most Americans had never even heard of. But the campaign triggered by that attack would take U.S. troops thousands of miles across the globe.

While most U.S. Army divisions were directed toward the action in Europe, the United States Marine Corps was allocated for the campaign in the Pacific. The marines had long been deemed one of the most elite fighting forces in the world. Specializing in amphibious operations, the Marine Corps would prove vital to the American armed forces during World War II. In June 1941, before the outbreak of war, the Marine Corps maintained a refined and limited 54,000 troops. By the time the marines embarked on their first Pacific campaign in 1942, they numbered nearly 150,000. The average age of a United States Marine at the time was just 18 years old. The marines sought vengeance against an enemy that had outraged every single American man, woman, and child.

The first step on the marines' path to Japan was Guadalcanal, one of the Solomon Islands in the western Pacific Ocean. The Marine Corps made their first amphibious landing at Guadalcanal on August 7, 1942. Some 6,000 troops faced a garrison of more than 2,000 Japanese defenders. The campaign marked the first land offensive made by the Allies in the Pacific theater. It was also a valuable and costly lesson for the United States, which had no prior experience against an enemy as determined as the Japanese. After the American victory on Guadalcanal, Allied military leaders devised an island-hopping campaign that would take their forces directly to the Japanese main islands. But it would be a long and costly journey through dense and inhospitable jungle, brutal heat, and widespread disease, all while battling a determined and fanatical foe.

The Battle of the Philippine Sea

More than two years after Guadalcanal, the Japanese forces were still feverishly defending every island that led to their mainland. Meanwhile, since their victory at Midway, the U.S. Navy continued to dominate the seas. The marines embarked on several amphibious assaults across the region, including the Marshall Islands and the Mariana Islands—volcanic island chains vital to Japan's security. The most notable campaigns were on Saipan and its neighboring island Tinian. These islands had airfields that, if captured, would put the Americans in range to bomb the Japanese home islands.

In late June 1944, as U.S. Marines fought for control of the Marianas, the Imperial Japanese Navy made its last major stand against the Americans in the Philippine Sea. After a string of devastating defeats, Japan's naval leaders planned a final large-scale attack that they hoped would turn the war in their favor. The Pacific campaign relied heavily on amphibious warfare, and it was clear that the side that controlled the seas would emerge victorious. On the eve of the battle, Japanese admiral Soemu Toyoda, commander of the Combined Fleet, declared, "The fate of the Empire rests on this one battle."

On June 19, 1944, the Japanese clashed with the U.S. Navy in the Battle of the Philippine Sea. The engagement would become the most significant carrier battle of the war. Like the Battle of the Coral Sea and the Battle of Midway, much of the action was fought in the air. And despite their best attempts to destroy the superior American fleet, Japan's air and sea forces floundered. American carrier-based fighters decimated the Japanese fleet in what would become known as the "Marianas Turkey Shoot." By the end of the battle, U.S. naval aviators shot down between 550 and 645 enemy aircraft, losing 123 of their own planes in the process. In addition, three Japanese aircraft carriers, the *Shokaku*, *Hiryu*, and *Taiho*, were torpedoed by American submarines. These losses sealed the outcome of the battle and the eventual fate of the Marianas. Japanese prime minister Hideki Tojo resigned after the battle, humiliated and disgraced by the defeat. By the evening of June 20, the Japanese were once again in retreat.

With yet another victory at sea, the United States resumed its operations on Saipan, penetrating deeper into the island. Approximately 5,000 U.S. troops died in the fighting, and nearly 23,000 Japanese defenders were killed. In addition, rather than facing capture, thousands of Japanese civilians and soldiers committed suicide by jumping to their death at "Banzai Cliff." Within a month, the islands of Tinian and Guam were captured as well. The United States now had access to airfields that could be used in the bombardment of the Japanese mainland. The Battle of the Philippine Sea was a significant step toward the destruction of Japan's air and sea forces. Still, the Japanese admiralty was not prepared to admit defeat.

The Battle of Leyte Gulf

By autumn of 1944, American and Japanese forces had been fighting in the Pacific for three years. Following the clash in the Philippine Sea, America's dominance in the air and on the seas was nearly secured. The Japanese had lost close to 500 planes and several aircraft carriers, severely weakening their ability to wage war. The remainder of Japan's navy mostly comprised battleships and heavy cruisers. These formidable surface vessels were a strong match to their U.S. navy counterparts. Among the Japanese fleet were the *Musashi* and *Yamato*, the largest battleships ever built. Known as "super-battleships," these massive vessels were more than 862 feet long and 121 feet wide, and weighed more than 70,000 tons fully loaded. Heavily armored and surprisingly quick, the ships were the pride of the Imperial Japanese Navy.

Meanwhile, the Americans had mastered the art of carrier warfare. By mid-October, U.S. military leaders had planned an amphibious invasion of the Philippines, beginning at the centrally located island of Leyte. Japan had conquered the Philippines in 1942. This allowed them to establish a vital sea route to obtain essential resources for war, such as rubber and petroleum. When U.S. Army General Douglas MacArthur was forced out of the Philippines, leaving 90,000 American and Filipino troops behind, he famously promised, "I shall return."

On October 20, 1944, American forces landed on Leyte, the first step in the liberation of the entire Philippine archipelago. With the tide of the war now turning in his favor, MacArthur was finally ready to deliver on his promise. Following the news of the invasion, Japan's battleships and cruisers steamed toward Leyte to disrupt the American beach landings. But unlike previous sea engagements in the Pacific, the Japanese didn't target American battleships. Instead, they attacked transports and landing craft to destroy the logistical aspect of the invasion. When the two navies met on October 23, the Battle of Leyte Gulf began. This would be the largest naval battle in history. The Japanese caught the Americans off guard, and the U.S. Navy was severely outnumbered and desperately outgunned. But they wouldn't go down without a fight.

AMERICAN LANDING CRAFT AT THE BATTLE OF LEYTE GULF, OCTOBER 1944

The Americans rallied their forces, counterattacking against the superior Japanese fleet. Lightly armed destroyers charged the mighty Japanese armada. Hundreds of American aircraft swarmed in from above, relentlessly bombing and strafing the enemy ships. The U.S. destroyers launched torpedoes, sinking and damaging several vessels. Smoke screens and other tactical distractions caused mass confusion for the Japanese commanders, who were constantly maneuvering their ships to avoid air attacks. With the battle now taking a drastic turn, the Japanese introduced kamikazes, suicide bombers tasked to fly directly into American ships. These pilots were used in large numbers, and they inflicted heavy casualties on the U.S. fleet. An estimated 5,000 kamikaze pilots died over the course of the battle.

UP FOR DEBATE: THE KAMIKAZES

In the final months of the war, the Japanese grew desperate to defend their homeland. They deployed suicide pilots, or kamikazes, who sacrificed their lives for their emperor and their country. In Japan, it was considered an honor to die in service of your nation. The kamikazes became a natural part of their radical culture. The average suicide pilot was just 21 years old and was revered in Japan. But to Americans, such a sacrifice was appalling and barbaric. Even decades after the war, the legacy of these suicide bombers is conflicted, and opinions on their morality and effectiveness are widely debated.

On October 24, the super-battleship *Musashi* was sunk by an estimated 19 torpedo hits and 17 bomb hits from American carrier-based aircraft. By October 26, with his fleet in shambles, the Japanese admiral in command decided he had had enough. He turned his remaining ships around and withdrew. The Japanese were ultimately defeated at Leyte Gulf. Their losses included four aircraft carriers, three battleships, 10 cruisers, nine destroyers, and more than 10,000 sailors and aircrewmen. For the remainder of the conflict, Japan was unable to muster enough force to repel any attacks from the U.S. Navy. Leyte was the last major sea battle of the war. The Imperial Japanese Navy, a force that once ruled the Pacific, had finally been eliminated through a series of key battles in a matter of months.

The Battle of Luzon

After the American naval victory at the Battle of Leyte Gulf, General MacArthur's army continued its land invasion of the Philippines. Throughout October 1944, more than 100,000 American soldiers landed on Leyte. They soon began one of the bloodiest battles of the Pacific War. MacArthur made good on his promise to return to the Philippines, and newsreels showed him triumphantly wading ashore from a landing craft on the first day of the assault. It took 67 days to secure the island, and more than 55,000 Japanese soldiers perished. U.S. deaths numbered close to 3,500. In late December, the Americans captured the island of Mindoro, giving the U.S. Army Air Forces a secure location to launch its aircraft in the upcoming invasion of Luzon.

On January 9, 1945, a massive bombardment marked the start of the Battle of Luzon. Home to Manila, the nation's capital, Luzon is the largest island in the Philippines. A large fleet carrying 175,000 troops waited offshore. On the first day, more than 60,000 U.S. soldiers landed during the Invasion of Lingayen Gulf, accompanied once again by General Douglas MacArthur. At first, American troops met little resistance, but kamikazes did succeed in striking the cruiser USS *Columbia* and battleship USS *Mississippi*. As American soldiers marched inland, the Japanese hid inside an elaborate network of caves that stretched throughout the island. The concealed Japanese survived the bombardment mostly unscathed. They also drew the American forces inland, and then attacked vigorously from the protection of these defensive strongholds. This proved to be a solid strategy used by the Japanese in many Pacific battles that followed. On January 15, a second, smaller invasion took place on Luzon, 45 miles from the capital. Manila was the most populated city in Southeast Asia at the time, and a bitter campaign was waged to capture the region. The Japanese fought savagely to defend it from the Americans. Much of the city was reduced to rubble by tanks, artillery, and other heavy weaponry used by both sides.

In the final weeks of the battle, the Japanese faced defeat on all fronts. They retaliated against the civilian population in what is now known as the Manila Massacre. Japanese soldiers committed mass atrocities, including rape, murder, and executions. An estimated 100,000 civilians lost their lives. Fighting to take Manila would last until March of 1945, when Allied forces finally secured the city. A total of 10 U.S. divisions would see combat on Luzon, making it the largest campaign in the Pacific theater. Military casualties on both sides were high, with more than 230,000 Japanese and 10,000 American soldiers losing their lives. Japan's defeat in the Battle of Luzon was soon followed by the complete U.S. liberation of the Philippines. With each battle won, the Americans were inching closer toward Japan home islands and the collapse of the Japanese Empire.

ARMS AND ARMOR: THE JAPANESE A6M ZERO

Japan's most famous fighter plane of World War II was the A6M Zero, a single-engine aircraft widely used across the Pacific theater. Manufactured by Mitsubishi Heavy Industries, the Zero was one of the most modern aircraft designs when it was introduced in 1940. With a top speed of 350 miles per hour, it could outmaneuver any other fighter in the world at the time. It was armed with four machine guns and could carry two bombs under its wings. In the early years of the war, the Zero was most commonly used as a carrier-based aircraft and made up much of the strike force in the attack on Pearl Harbor. In the last few months of the war, many Zeros were used in kamikaze attacks, once again proving their effectiveness in battle.

CHAPTER 5

THE MEDITERRANEAN AND NORTH AFRICA

After suffering humiliating losses in western Europe, the Allies were given a chance at redemption in North Africa. In the deserts of Egypt and Libya, they fought and eventually defeated the Germans. Just months later, British and American forces were fighting on Axis soil as they launched invasions into the heart of Fascist Italy. Lessons learned in these frequently overlooked campaigns would prove essential to Allied victory in Europe during World War II.

★ ★ ★

The Importance of Africa

Following the disastrous defeat on the Western Front in 1940, the Allies now battled for control of another theater of war: North Africa. When Italy declared war on Great Britain on June 10, 1940, skirmishes in the desert began almost immediately. Italian forces were stationed in their colony of Libya, while the British stood at the ready in their neighboring territory of Egypt. A British colony since 1882, Egypt was where the Suez Canal was located and served as a vital trade route for Great Britain. But North Africa was strategically important to both sides. The Italians sought control of the British and French colonies in Africa and wanted to seize the Suez Canal to gain access to Middle Eastern oil. Both sides maintained highly mechanized armies, and therefore oil was one of the most essential resources to control. Many of the Italian troops in Libya were young and heavily indoctrinated, so they were taught to believe that their enemies were inferior and would be easily defeated. When Italian dictator Benito Mussolini told Hitler about his plans to attack Egypt, Hitler offered German military assistance. But Mussolini declined. He believed Italy could take on the British alone.

On September 13, 1940, Italian forces stationed in Libya attacked Egypt, beginning the war in North Africa. Mussolini was convinced the attack would give Italy "glory" and establish its dominance and position as a new Roman Empire. But despite their advantage in numbers, the Italians had limited success. Plagued by poor leadership, lack of training, and outdated weapons, the Italian army was able to advance just 65 miles into Egypt before they were brought to a halt by determined British defenders. The war in the desert was defined by rugged terrain and an inhospitable climate. Less than two months later, a successful British counterattack drove deep into Italian territory, capturing the city of Tobruk in eastern Libya. Caught off guard and ill-prepared, some 130,000 Italian troops were captured.

With his Italian ally facing an inevitable defeat, Adolf Hitler sent the Deutsches Afrika Korps (German Africa Corps) to Libya. Commanded by General Erwin Rommel, the Afrika Korps rapidly changed the tide of the campaign against the British. Rommel was a highly respected and talented officer who had a distinguished reputation on the battlefield. After a series of victories in North Africa, he quickly gained the respect of his troops and his adversaries, and earned the nickname "the Desert Fox."

On March 24, 1941, Rommel and his army launched their first offensive against British forces in North Africa. In a swift action heavily supported by tanks, they bypassed Tobruk and reached the Egyptian border by mid-April. Several months passed with little activity as both sides remained in a stalemate. In July of 1941 when Germany invaded the Soviet Union, much of Rommel's army was diverted to Europe. Recognizing the Afrika Korps' weakened state, the British organized the Eighth Army in Egypt and launched a series of attacks on Rommel's positions.

Commanded by General Alan Cunningham, the Eighth Army was a diverse force. It was made up of British, Australian, Indian, South African, New Zealand, and Free French Troops. Despite early success in pushing the Germans back into Libya, a significant setback came when Japan attacked British territories in the Pacific on December 7 and 8, 1941. Much-needed troops in North Africa were diverted to defend British interests in Asia, leaving Egypt's defenses weakened. Meanwhile, seeing early victories in Russia, Hitler sent fresh tanks and equipment to North Africa. This enabled General Rommel to launch a second offensive into Egypt on January 21, 1942. Within two weeks, the strengthened German and Italian forces regained their lost territory and were just miles from the British stronghold at Tobruk.

The Battle of Crete

In the spring of 1941, as Rommel's panzers rolled across Africa, Italian and German forces in the Mediterranean fought to capture Greece, Yugoslavia, and Bulgaria. Italy had first invaded Greece in October 1940 but was pushed back by strong resistance the following March. As in North Africa, the German army came to the rescue. They launched their invasion of Greece on April 6, 1941. The Greeks were quickly overrun, and German forces reached the capital of Athens by April 27. With the Greek mainland lost, 57,000 British and Greek soldiers were evacuated by the Royal Navy to the island of Crete. "Creforce," as they came to be known, was commanded by New Zealand Major General Bernard Freyberg. He was given the difficult task of defending Greece's largest island from the Germans.

Crete had immense tactical importance to the Allies. It could serve as a base for an invasion across the Balkans. It also gave the Royal Air Force landing strips to launch bombing raids on the Romanian oil fields, the German army's primary oil source. For the Axis powers, Crete could provide the Germans with a staging point for naval and air operations in the Mediterranean and support the ongoing battle in Egypt to capture the Suez Canal.

On May 20, 1941, Germany launched a daring airborne attack on Crete, using the elite Fallschirmjägers, a paratrooper force masterminded by Luftwaffe General Kurt Student. Thousands of paratroopers were flown in and dropped over Crete. Their mission was to capture the strategic airfields of Maleme, Rethymno, and Heraklion, so reinforcements could be supplied by air. The first wave of paratroopers landed on top of Allied positions. They suffered heavy casualties in hand-to-hand fighting, while others were shot and killed before they even reached the ground. The second wave of

Fallschirmjägers dropped later that day. They also suffered heavy losses, and many transport aircraft were shot down. The German invasion appeared to be a costly failure. By the end of the first day, they had not captured any of their objectives.

But the British were also facing difficulties. Allied communications had broken down, which resulted in confusion and disorganization among the troops on the island. In addition, the mountainous terrain proved difficult to defend. The British had no aircraft and only a handful of tanks. After the first day of parachutist landings, Major General Freyberg anticipated a German assault from the sea and ordered his forces to meet this threat. This left the vital airfield at Maleme exposed on its western side. On the second day of the battle, the German paratroopers counterattacked and seized control of the lightly defended airfield. Although they faced constant harassment from British artillery and small-arms fire, German troop carriers were now able to land and disembark reinforcements.

Freyberg's critical miscalculation marked the turning point in the Battle of Crete. British forces fought on for several more days, but it soon became apparent that their struggle was in vain. On May 27, Freyberg ordered an evacuation from the island, once again tasking the Royal Navy with saving a defeated British army. Between May 28 and June 1, 1941, 18,000 troops were evacuated. More than 4,000 British, Australian, and New Zealand soldiers were killed, and more than 11,000 were captured. Despite their humiliating defeat, the British had severely battered the German attackers, killing more than 3,000 paratroopers. The Germans never attempted a major airborne operation for the rest of the war. Hitler declared to General Student, "The day of the parachutist is over."

The Battle of El Alamein and Operation Torch

Back in North Africa, General Rommel and the Afrika Korps had defeated the British at the Libyan village of Gazala and the oasis of Bir Hakeim. On May 26, 1942, German and Italian troops launched Operation Venezia, an offensive that encircled Tobruk and forced the British Eighth Army back to the Egyptian border. Tobruk came back under Axis control on June 21, and more than 30,000 Allied soldiers were taken as prisoners of war. The British withdrew to El Alamein, a town on Egypt's Mediterranean coast. Rommel's forces pursued the retreating British troops deep into Egypt. Their battle was one of the most decisive of the North African campaign. By July of 1942, the British had halted Rommel's advance at El Alamein and were holding their ground.

A GERMAN 88MM GUN OPERATING AS ANTI-TANK ARTILLERY AT THE BATTLE OF EL ALAMEIN, NORTH AFRICA, 1942

It was then that British prime minister Winston Churchill, despite the current military leadership's success, decided to replace all of his military commanders in North Africa. He appointed Lieutenant General Bernard Law Montgomery as commander of the Eighth Army. Montgomery received fresh troops and supplies, including American-manufactured tanks. With the Eighth Army replenished and once again ready for battle, Montgomery prepared to attack Rommel's forces at El Alamein.

ARMS AND ARMOR: THE AMERICAN M4 SHERMAN TANK

The M4 Sherman was America's main battle tank of World War II. It saw action in every theater of war from North Africa to the Pacific. Named after Civil War general William Tecumseh Sherman, the M4 was mass-produced to meet the needs of the growing American and British armed forces. The first Shermans went into combat with the British Army at El Alamein in 1942, proving to be a reliable and lethal weapon. Most M4s were armed with 75-millimeter cannons along with several Browning machine guns. Although they were often outgunned by their German counterparts, M4 Shermans were far easier to maintain and were deployed in greater numbers; nearly 50,000 were built over the course of the war.

On the evening of October 23, 1942, the attack commenced when Allied forces launched a massive artillery and aerial bombardment of Axis lines. When the bombing subsided, British troops began their advance, marching through the thick smoke that blanketed the desert battlefield. In the early hours of the assault, British soldiers penetrated deep into the

German minefields around El Alamein. Meanwhile, armored units struggled to attack fortified positions. When the fighting began, Rommel was away on sick leave in Germany. He quickly returned, but it was already too late. The Allied forces, led by General Montgomery, outnumbered the Germans almost two to one. The advantage in men and ammunition proved overwhelming and devastating to the Afrika Korps. Just 10 days after the battle began, Rommel was forced to retreat rapidly across Libya. According to Churchill, El Alamein was "a glorious and decisive victory." Back home in Britain, church bells were rung for the first time since May 1940 in celebration of the Eighth Army's success.

Rommel's retreat coincided with Allied amphibious landings west of the fighting at El Alamein. On November 8, 1942, a combined Anglo-American force launched Operation Torch. Troops landed on the shores of present-day Morocco and Algeria, territories controlled by Vichy France, a puppet state of Nazi Germany. The Allied forces were tasked with capturing important naval docks and airports at Casablanca, Oran, and Algiers. Next, they were to advance eastward into Tunisia to face the Afrika Korps. British Intelligence suggested that the French would surrender their positions without a fight, but the 125,000 Vichy troops stationed in northwestern Africa offered stubborn resistance. Moderate losses were suffered on the shores of Morocco, and a short but fierce naval engagement took place off Casablanca, during which the French lost a battleship, a light cruiser, and several destroyers and submarines. Despite the initial ferocity of the French defense, the British and American forces quickly pushed inland. By November 11, Admiral Jean-François Darlan, the Vichy high commissioner for North Africa, ordered his forces to stand down. For the Allies, the valuable lessons learned would set the framework for future amphibious assaults throughout the rest of the war.

Operation Torch is one of the forgotten invasions of World War II, but its impact and importance in the North African campaign and on the war as a whole deserve to be remembered. It opened a second front for German and Italian forces already battling the British in Libya and Egypt. Now trapped between two Allied armies, Rommel's retreat across the desert ground to a halt. Torch marked the first major combined British and American invasion in North Africa. It also provided relief for the Red Army on the Eastern Front by diverting Axis forces to North Africa. It is estimated that half of the Luftwaffe transport planes needed to resupply the encircled troops at Stalingrad were tied up supporting German forces in North Africa. Victory at El Alamein, combined with the success of Operation Torch, forced the Axis to surrender in North Africa by May 1943.

The Italian Campaign

With victory secured in North Africa, the Allies now looked to invade Europe and bring the war to Hitler's doorstep. At the Casablanca Conference in January 1943, Allied leaders decided to invade Italy. British prime minister Winston Churchill called Italy part of "the soft underbelly of Europe." The Italian military had been severely depleted by their losses in North Africa, and Allied military leaders believed the time had come to strike the final blow against Mussolini and his Fascist nation. The main goal of an invasion of Italy was to remove the regime from the war and eliminate one of the Axis powers. But the British and Americans also hoped that Germany would rush to defend its ally. They hoped that Hitler would divert troops from the Eastern Front and, more importantly, from northern France, where the Allies were planning to launch their main invasion of Europe.

In April 1943, in the final month of the North African campaign, Spanish fishermen discovered the body of a British

THE 1ST CANADIAN INFANTRY DIVISION AT THE INVASION AND LIBERATION OF SICILY, JULY 1943

Royal Marine pilot lying in waters off the southern coast of Spain. The officer had a briefcase chained to his wrist that contained top secret papers relating to an Allied invasion of Italy on the islands of Sardinia and Corsica. Spain was purportedly a neutral nation during World War II. Nonetheless, the Spanish government retrieved the documents and shared copies with the *Abwehr*, Germany's military intelligence organization, before returning the originals to the British. The plans soon reached Adolf Hitler, who carefully studied the captured documents and took full advantage of their details. He then sent substantial reinforcements to Sardinia and Corsica to meet the Allied invasion.

But there was one major problem. The plans and even the identity of the body were all part of an elaborate hoax known as Operation Mincemeat. The drowned Royal Marine officer, who the Germans identified as "William Martin," was actually a homeless man named Glyndwr Michael, who had committed suicide some months earlier. In one of the most successful deceptions ever achieved in the history of warfare, British intelligence officers planted his corpse on the Spanish coast, complete with a new identity and forged invasion plans. The *Abwehr* fell for the trick and considered the discovery to be of great importance to the war effort.

On July 10, 1943, American and British airborne and amphibious forces landed on the southern coast of Sicily. This was Italy's largest and southernmost island in the Mediterranean. Code-named Operation Husky, the invasion involved more than 150,000 soldiers, some 3,000 ships, and 4,000 aircraft. Hitler had been so deceived by Operation Mincemeat that he left only two German divisions to defend Sicily. Even as the invasion got underway, he believed it was just a diversion to distract the Germans from the main landing at Sardinia or Corsica. But it was soon clear that Operation Husky was the real thing. Thousands of American and British soldiers poured onto the island.

Meanwhile, just as the Allies had hoped, the Italian Fascist regime was falling into disarray. On July 25, 1943, Italian dictator Benito Mussolini was overthrown and arrested. Marshal Pietro Badoglio took power and immediately began secret negotiations with the Allies. With foreign troops now on Italian soil, Hitler canceled a major offensive in Russia and diverted the forces to Italy. On July 25, just one day after Mussolini's arrest, Italian defenses on Sicily crumbled and began retreating toward the northeastern port of Messina. German troops remained vigilant, digging into the mountainous terrain and attacking the British and American invaders from above.

Throughout late July and early August, Allied troops on the island battled the determined German defenders. The Allies closed in on the coastal town of Messina, eager to destroy the fleeing Axis forces. But when the first American soldiers reached Messina on August 17, 1943, they were surprised to find that the enemy forces had disappeared. Over a period of several days, the Axis armies had managed to evacuate nearly 100,000 soldiers to the Italian mainland along with their tanks, vehicles, and ammunition. The Allies had achieved a swift victory on Sicily, but their failure to capture the fleeing German and Italian troops undermined their success. When Sicily fell, the Germans sent 16 new divisions to the Italian mainland to defend against the impending Allied invasion.

The Battle of Monte Cassino

At this point in the war, the Italian government had overthrown Mussolini and surrendered its armed forces to the Allies. But the country was now occupied and defended by the Germans, who were determined to hold the Italian mainland. Luftwaffe Field Marshal Albert Kesselring was placed in charge of the defense. Hitler commanded him to make the Allies pay for every inch of their advance. As part of his plan to fortify the country, Kesselring constructed a series of defensive lines that stretched across the narrow Italian peninsula. The rivers, mountains, and rocky terrain of Italy made it an ideal place for such positions. Natural fortifications were supported by vast minefields, machine-gun nests, and artillery positions. The largest and most notable German defensive formation was the Gustav Line, an elevated position entrenched in the mountains.

The Allied military leaders faced a formidable task when planning their assault of the Italian mainland. They eventually decided to launch the invasion using three sep-arate amphibious assaults. The first attack commenced on September 3, 1943, when the British Eighth Army crossed the Strait of Messina from Sicily and landed at Calabria. Six days later, on September 9, General Mark Clark's Fifth U.S. Army landed at Salerno, meeting stiff resistance as they fought to establish a beachhead. The strong German defenses nearly succeeded in driving the American invasion force back into the Tyrrhenian Sea.

At approximately the same time, the British 1st Airborne Division came ashore at Taranto. British troops had early success with their assaults and forced the German defenders on a slow retreat. By the end of September, Allied forces had reached Naples and pushed inland toward the north. The nonstop fighting was compounded by heavy rains that washed out roads, flooded rivers, and turned fields into mud. The U.S. Fifth and British Eighth Armies were both highly mechanized units, but their vehicles were hampered by the rough Italian terrain. Winston Churchill's claim that Italy was part of "the soft underbelly of Europe" proved far from reality. Instead, the Allies were faced with what General Mark Clark called "a tough old gut."

By the end of 1943, British and American forces had pushed the Germans back to the strongest of their defensive lines: the Gustav Line. But Kesselring's tactical advantage, combined with poor weather, halted the Allied offensive. At the center of the Gustav Line was the mountain of Monte Cassino, whose peak was dominated by a 1,400-year-old Benedictine abbey. The abbey was of great historical importance, and both the Germans and the Allies had assured the Vatican that it would not be attacked or put to military use. As the battle progressed, constant artillery fire rained down on the Allied troops, inflicting heavy casualties. Due to the accuracy of the strikes, Allied leaders believed that the Germans had occupied the abbey and were using it to direct fire. Despite the lack of evidence and the fact that Monte Cassino was a protected site, on February 15, 1944, American bombers dropped more than 1,150 tons of explosives on the ancient structure and the surrounding town, reducing it to rubble. It was later discovered that the abbey had not been used by the Germans until after the air strikes, when the ruins provided an even more formidable defensive position. The Allies continued their attempts to breach the Gustav Line but were repeatedly unsuccessful until May 1944, when the Germans were compelled to retreat northward.

MATTER OF CHOICE: BOMBING THE ABBEY

When the abbey of Monte Cassino was leveled by Allied bombers in February 1944, questions about the destruction soon arose. After the war, the Allies insisted the bombing was justified and that there was "irrefutable" evidence the building was used as part of the German defenses. However, a 1949 report on the incident concluded that no such evidence existed; the abbey was not occupied by German forces during the bombing. This information was kept hidden from the public until 1969, nearly 25 years after the attack. However, the decision to bomb the abbey was made under tremendous stress in a combat zone, where the importance of human life outweighed that of a building, no matter how historically significant. Regardless, the tragic destruction of Monte Cassino is considered to be one of the greatest cultural losses of World War II.

The Battle of Anzio

When the invasion of Italy began in September of 1943, Allied leaders were optimistic about a quick victory. But by January 1944, the end was still not in sight. German forces at the Gustav Line maintained their defense, and the Allies struggled to mount offensives to capture the abbey of Monte Cassino.

On January 22, in an attempt to outflank the German forces and pave the way for an attack on Rome, the Allies launched

Operation Shingle. This would be an amphibious assault at Anzio on Italy's western coast. General Mark Clark, the U.S. Fifth Army commander, knew that for the invasion to be a success, the landing force had to disembark and move inland as quickly as possible. They needed to avoid encirclement by German forces, which were positioned just miles away. While Clark certainly understood the risk and essential factors of the operation, he failed to pass the information on to his subordinate, Major General John P. Lucas, commander of the invasion force at Anzio.

When the assault commenced, the landing forces encountered light resistance. And while General Lucas achieved

BRITISH SOLDIERS ADVANCING ACROSS SNOW-COVERED MOUNTAINS AFTER THE ANZIO LANDINGS, ITALY 1944

the element of surprise, he failed to take advantage of it. Instead, he ordered his troops to dig in, delaying his advance until all of his units had landed and were organized on the beach. Meanwhile, German Field Marshal Albert Kesselring moved every available unit he could find to form a defensive ring that completely surrounded the beachhead. The Allied troops were now besieged at Anzio. They endured constant artillery, mortar, and small-arms fire. After a month of heavy fighting, Lucas was relieved of his command and replaced by Major General Lucian Truscott, who took a more active approach to the invasion. It took the Allies until May 1944 to finally establish the upper hand at Anzio and begin their breakout into Italy.

UP FOR DEBATE: THE ALLIED LANDING AT ANZIO

The Allied landings at Anzio in January 1944 were intended to deliver a surprise blow to the German forces and bring an end to the long and bloody struggle to take the Gustav Line. When the first Allied troops landed, they met little resistance. But German field marshal Albert Kesselring was quick to react. He had anticipated such a move and promptly sent reinforcements to Anzio, trapping the outnumbered Allied force on the beach. It took several months of bitter fighting for the American and British troops to finally break out. While the battle was ultimately considered a victory, it was one of the most poorly planned and executed operations of the war. Opinions about the importance and outcome of Anzio are conflicting, but most historians agree that the plan was doomed from the start.

Around the same time, the Polish 2nd Corps succeeded in capturing Monte Cassino. Kesselring's defenses along the Gustav Line had started to falter. The fall of Monte Cassino opened the road to Rome and marked the beginning of the end of the German occupation of Italy. Once the breakout at Anzio had succeeded, General Clark decided to turn his forces to the northwest. Instead of heading inland to assist the Allied units at Monte Cassino, he headed toward Rome, the capital of Italy. This allowed close to 100,000 German soldiers who were retreating from Monte Cassino to escape capture and rebuild their defensive positions farther north. Clark's decision ended up prolonging the Italian campaign by months. His willingness to put personal glory above his soldiers was incredibly controversial and made him an unpopular figure among the troops fighting in the region.

General Clark's forces entered Rome on June 4, 1944. "The Eternal City" was the first Axis capital to fall to the Allies. It was a huge propaganda victory, but the achievement was largely overshadowed by the Allied invasion in France that took place two days later, on June 6, when the Allies landed on the beaches of Normandy. Soon after, operations in France took priority over the Italian campaign, and several divisions were diverted to take part in the drive to Berlin. For the remainder of the war, British and U.S. forces in Italy were tasked with pinning down as many German divisions as possible rather than continuing offensive operations. This controversial strategy ultimately succeeded in forcing the Germans to keep a large number of troops in the Mediterranean, making the Allied task easier in other theaters. Fighting in Italy continued until the German forces finally surrendered on May 2, 1945, six days before victory in Europe was declared. More than 300,000 Allied troops in Italy had been killed, missing, or wounded in action. German casualties totaled around 434,000.

CHAPTER 6

THE FINAL THROES OF WAR IN EUROPE

From the beaches of Normandy to the streets of Berlin, the last battles of World War II in Europe toppled the Third Reich in a dramatic climax. The war's end exposed appalling atrocities that shocked the world. The journey to victory over Nazism was both long and destructive, but the triumphant will and determination of the Allied armies made way for the return of freedom and democracy across Europe.

The Long Road to France

On June 6, 1944, the first Allied troops landed on the coast of France in an operation that would become famously known as D-Day. But to understand the full story of this monumental invasion, we must travel back to 1940, four years before the Allied landings.

On May 10, 1940, Germany invaded France. Within six weeks, Paris had fallen, and the government capitulated. As early as 1942, Allied leaders considered a major invasion across the English Channel to liberate France and open a front against the Germans. However, they chose to attack Italy first, intending to open an easy route into Germany. After the successful campaigns in North Africa and Sicily, hopes were high for the quick capture of the Italian mainland and a subsequent drive into southern Germany. But as British and American troops grew bogged down in the fighting, it soon became clear that the campaign in Italy wasn't going to be easy. With their advance stalled, Allied leaders gave the green light to open a second front in Europe: the invasion of Nazi-occupied France.

The Germans were well aware that the Allies intended to invade France, but they did not know where or when it would occur. Field Marshal Erwin Rommel was in command of the German forces in northern France. He firmly believed that the only way Germany could defeat the invading force was to destroy it before it got ashore. In an attempt to defend the shores of German-occupied French territory, Hitler ordered the construction of the Atlantic Wall. This was an elaborate series of coastal fortifications and beach defenses that stretched 2,000 miles from the northern tip of Norway to France's border with Spain. (Spain was a neutral country in World War II.) Further, Rommel gave orders to build anti-invasion obstacles on the beaches. These included mines and anti-tank defenses known as "hedgehogs." Beginning in 1942, thousands of reinforced bunkers and pillboxes—concrete structures that housed firearms and troops—were constructed by more than 230,000 enslaved laborers and prisoners of war. This forced labor was under the supervision of Organisation Todt, Nazi Germany's civil and military engineering group. Their constant and grueling work under unimaginable conditions was the backbone of one of the largest construction projects in history. By the summer of 1944, more than 15,000 bunkers lined the coast of Europe, defended by 300,000 troops. Today, many of these structures remain a reminder of the Nazi occupation of France and the eventual liberation by Allied forces.

MATTER OF CHOICE: THE LESSONS LEARNED AT DIEPPE

On August 19, 1942, the Allies launched Operation Jubilee, an amphibious attack on the German-occupied fishing port of Dieppe in northern France. It tested the possibility of a large-scale beach landing in western Europe. The attack was designed to infiltrate and destroy critical military targets, including German coastal defenses and port facilities. The raiding force consisted mainly of Canadian infantry supported by a regiment of tanks and British Royal Air Force fighters. The Dieppe Raid was nothing short of a disaster. The tanks were stuck on the beach, and the infantry were forced to fight on alone, unable to achieve their objectives. Within hours of landing, more than half of the 6,086 men who had gone ashore were killed, wounded, or captured as prisoners of war. Despite the horrific losses, some historians credit the failure at Dieppe as an important learning experience for the Allied forces. The costly lessons learned at Dieppe became valuable in planning the successful D-Day landings two years later.

By the spring of 1944, Great Britain had rebuilt its military, and a massive American army was quartered on its shores, poised and prepared to assault Hitler's "Fortress Europe." The Germans were still unaware of when and where the invasion would occur, but it was commonly believed that the Allies would land in the Pas-de-Calais region, where the distance across the English Channel was the shortest. The Germans made this the most heavily fortified area of the Atlantic Wall. However, the Allies, under the command of American general Dwight D. Eisenhower, had other plans. They would strike in Normandy, one of France's northernmost regions. Normandy was also the farthest distance across the channel. The Germans considered Normandy a highly unlikely target for an invasion. In the months leading up to D-Day, the Allies launched air attacks against railways, roads, and bridges across France to hinder German efforts to move reinforcements to the coast.

Simultaneously, an elaborate deception was underway that fooled the Germans and "confirmed" that Pas-de-Calais would be the target of the Allied attack. While the real invasion force trained and prepared opposite the Normandy coast, a "ghost army" was created across from Pas-de-Calais. Fictional units were formed, replica tanks and planes were erected, and notable generals such as George S. Patton were assigned to command them. Inflatable rubber tanks and artillery were assembled in large numbers, along with hundreds of plywood replicas of aircraft. The phony equipment was placed in camps across the coast in clear view of German aerial reconnaissance. Loudspeakers were also used to simulate sounds of tanks, troops, and aircraft. The deception was a huge success, and the Germans were confident that these fictional units were the main bulk of the Allied landing force.

As the Allies worked to maintain secrecy, the Germans were facing problems of their own. Hitler had warned his generals that an Allied offensive on the Western Front could come as early as autumn 1943 and no later than the spring of 1944. But as spring came and went, and no Allied invasion arrived, the situation grew increasingly tense. The Germans were still constructing new Atlantic Wall defenses while troops waited in bunkers up and down the French coast. Making matters worse, the two men charged with defending France had fundamental disagreements over tank placement. Field Marshal Gerd von Rundstedt, commander in chief of German forces in the west, believed that the panzers should be kept inland. Once the Allied invasion began, they could be routed to a specific location to meet the threat. Erwin Rommel, who had been promoted by Hitler to field marshal after capturing Tobruk in 1942, adamantly disagreed. He argued that the panzers should be placed along the beaches to attack the landing forces straightaway. The North African campaign had taught Rommel that without air superiority, which the Germans didn't have in either campaign, moving tanks across open country was a near-impossible task. But Von Rundstedt was Rommel's superior, and consequently the German panzer reserves remained miles inland.

In early June 1944, the weather over the English Channel was bad, with high winds and heavy rain. Rommel was convinced that the Allies would not dare to cross under such conditions and went home to Germany to celebrate his wife's birthday. Despite the risks, Eisenhower felt that D-Day had arrived. The invasion of Normandy, code-named Operation Overlord, was about to begin.

The Invasion of Normandy

Today, the beaches of Normandy are quiet and peaceful. Tall grass sways in the breeze, sunlight sparkles on the water, and birds fly gracefully along the shoreline. But in 1944, Normandy witnessed one of the bloodiest battles of World War II.

By early June, Eisenhower was eager to launch the invasion of France. D-Day was initially scheduled for June 5, but poor weather conditions forced Eisenhower to postpone the invasion for 24 hours. Although the weather wasn't much better the next day, he decided to begin the invasion anyway. He feared that the element of surprise could be lost at any time. On June 6, 1944, Allied armies embarked upon the largest combined amphibious and airborne invasion in history. More than 150,000 men went ashore that day to liberate Europe, carried across the Channel by 4,100 vessels as nearly 11,500 aircraft flew overhead.

AMERICAN FORCES LAND AT OMAHA BEACH DURING THE INVASION OF NORMANDY, 1944

Five beaches in Normandy were designated for the Allied landing. They were code-named Omaha, Utah, Gold, Juno, and Sword. Omaha and Utah were given to the Americans, while Gold, Juno, and Sword were to be taken by British and

Canadian troops. This amphibious assault was supported by both American and British paratroopers who jumped into France the night before the invasion. Dropped behind enemy lines, the paratroopers were tasked with securing strategic targets and halting the advancing German troops. As the paratroopers dropped into the unknown, a mighty Allied armada was steaming toward the coast of France. The scene in the English Channel was beyond description. Thousands of vessels of every shape and size stretched as far as the eye could see. Thick mist and heavy fog extended over the horizon, and rough seas produced miserable conditions. Everyone anxiously waited to embark upon what General Eisenhower called "the Great Crusade."

As the troopships neared the shore, soldiers began climbing down cargo nets in order to board the landing crafts waiting in the waters below. As the small vessels set out toward the beach, Allied naval artillery announced the start of the invasion, bombing the German defenses. At approximately 6:30 a.m., the first wave of American troops landed at Omaha Beach. When the landing craft hit the shore and the ramps went down, machine-gun bullets ripped into the soldiers' bodies before they had a chance to disembark. German defenders had a clear line of fire from their elevated positions. They immediately started bombarding the American troops. Some soldiers jumped over the sides of their boats in a frantic attempt to make it ashore. Burdened by heavy equipment and ammunition, many drowned before they could reach the beach.

In the early hours of D-Day, thousands of small wooden landing craft known as Higgins boats headed for the coast of France. They transported the Allied troops ashore in the largest seaborne invasion in history. Officially known as an LCVP (landing craft, vehicle, personnel), the Higgins boat became iconic for the crucial role it played during the Normandy landings and at nearly every major amphibious operation during World War II. LCVPs were constructed mostly of plywood and featured a massive armored bow ramp that lowered upon reaching shore. The ramp allowed the 36 troops inside to rush off in a matter of seconds. More than 23,000 boats were manufactured by Higgins Industries in New Orleans, Louisiana, and are commonly referred to as "the boat that won the war." Today there are only nine known surviving original Higgins boats in the United States, out of only 19 worldwide.

The fighting at "Bloody Omaha" became the deadliest of all the beaches. The other landing sites saw fewer casualties, but the invasion would ultimately fail if Omaha could not be secured. American troops were pinned down on the beach for nearly two hours before they were finally able to break through the German defenses. Barbed wire, mines, and anti-tank obstacles reached all the way to the water's edge. Allied casualties on June 6, 1944, have been estimated at more than 10,000. On Omaha Beach alone, more than 4,700 Americans were killed, wounded, or missing in action. Today, much of the battlefield is untouched. The beaches of Normandy are sacred ground in France, and the people remain grateful to the brave soldiers who fought and died to liberate their country. But the beach landings on D-Day were just the beginning of a long and costly battle that was to come. From June 6 to August 21, the Allies landed more than two million soldiers in Normandy, initiating an enormous drive across France.

The Road to Victory

Throughout July and August 1944, the Allies fought to break out of Normandy. Combat was especially fierce in the hedgerows, a critical geographical feature not recognized by the Allies' aerial reconnaissance. Hedgerows are tall, thick shrubs that are supported by a dense base of dirt and rocks. For centuries, Norman farmers would pile debris from their fields onto the bottom of the hedgerows, creating almost wall-like barriers. The American soldiers struggled to overcome these formidable obstacles, which provided perfect cover for the Germans. It took several weeks, and a significant number of casualties, before the breakout was successful.

Meanwhile, the U.S. Army Air Force had begun a vast bombing campaign on targets of military importance to Nazi Germany. Factories, rail yards, and oil fields were bombed by massive formations of aircraft. Thousands of planes would strike a target at a single time, obliterating whatever lay below. The bombers were constantly harassed by thick German antiaircraft fire and Luftwaffe fighters. The Army Air Forces suffered the highest casualty rate of any other branch of the U.S. armed forces during World War II. More than 318,000 airmen had died by the end of the war. Despite the heavy losses, the raids successfully depleted German resources. In addition to military targets, cities were also bombed, inflicting large civilian casualties. The German people endured great hardship during the final years of the war as they were led under the guise of patriotism and loyalty to Adolf Hitler.

Back on the ground, the Americans were approaching Paris. Hitler ordered the city burned and all landmarks, including the Eiffel Tower, to be destroyed. But the German general in command of the defense ignored the order and spared France's historic capital. The Allies entered Paris in August 1944 facing minimal resistance. The city's residents poured into the streets to welcome their liberators and celebrate the end of the occupation. This Allied victory allowed France to regain its national pride and freedom and was an important step on the road to Berlin. On August 26, a huge demonstration was held in Paris, and the might of the Allies was put on parade in a triumphant march through the city. The liberation of France ultimately put the Allies within striking distance of Germany.

The Battle of the Bulge

After the invasion of France, the Allied armies advanced swiftly across Europe, faster than either the Allies or Germans had expected. Hitler was now faced with converging enemies on two fronts, and his Reich was beginning to fall apart. On the Eastern Front, Soviet forces were reoccupying massive amounts of land. Germany's Balkan territories, including Greece and Yugoslavia, were slowly being recaptured by determined resistance fighters. In the west, France, Belgium, and the Netherlands were liberated, and the Allies were holding ground in the thick Ardennes forest on the border with Germany. American commanders grew confident that they could reach Berlin by Christmas 1944 and swiftly end the war. But Allied troops were suffering from exhaustion after weeks of nonstop combat, and supplies were starting to run low. Due to this overconfidence, frontline positions were stretched dangerously thin. A lack of sufficient aerial reconnaissance failed to recognize the growing threat that was amassing in the distance. With his empire on the brink of collapse, Adolf Hitler devised a counteroffensive on American positions in the Ardennes, aiming to recapture the vital supply port of Antwerp and split the Allied front in two.

On the morning of December 16, 1944, the Germans launched Unternehmen Wacht am Rhein (Operation Watch on the Rhine). They sent nearly 200,000 troops and 1,000 tanks through the densely forested Ardennes in eastern Belgium, northeastern France, and Luxembourg. The operation was a total surprise to the Americans. Within days, American defenses had broken, and the Germans began their sweep back across western Europe. Hitler's forces had created a large triangular bulge that stretched deep into Allied lines, coining the commonly known name of Battle of the Bulge. The U.S. forces were ill-prepared for winter combat, lacking proper clothing, equipment, and ammunition. The Germans took advantage of foggy and cloudy weather, which grounded the superior Allied air force and gave the German panzers free rein on the ground.

German success in the Ardennes relied on speed and decisiveness, much like the blitzkrieg campaigns of 1939–41. To add to their superiority, the Germans organized units of English-speaking soldiers dressed in U.S. uniforms and sent them behind American lines to tamper with road signs and cut telephone wires. This caused mass confusion and resulted in many communication difficulties in the early days of the battle. As American troops rapidly retreated, they established defensive strongpoints at the Belgian towns of St. Vith and Bastogne. The entire 101st Airborne Division was entrapped inside Bastogne, holding out for seven days against ferocious German attacks.

By Christmas Eve 1944, the German advance had reached its peak. Fuel supplies were running low, and many tank crews were forced to abandon their equipment. General George S. Patton's Third Army relieved the 101st Airborne at Bastogne, and the skies cleared. American planes could now target German ground forces with great effectiveness. By late January, an American counteroffensive had regained all lost territory. Still, the impact of the Ardennes offensive was immense. The Americans suffered close to 90,000 casualties, including almost 20,000 fatalities and more than 23,000 missing in action, making the Battle of the Bulge the second-most-deadly American battle in history. This was a startling wake-up call for Allied leaders who had believed the war would be won by Christmas. The Battle of the Bulge proved that World War II in Europe was far from over.

A Horrific Discovery

As the Allies advanced on Germany from the west and the Soviets pushed toward Berlin from the east, soldiers found evidence of a genocide that had occurred largely unbeknownst to the world. They had discovered the Holocaust, Nazi

RECENTLY LIBERATED PRISONERS AT AUSCHWITZ-BIRKENAU CONCENTRATION CAMP, POLAND, 1945

Germany's state-sponsored persecution and eventual killing of six million European Jews. Since the beginning of the war, rumors had spread of war crimes committed by German forces. But what was uncovered surpassed all presumptions.

The origins of the Holocaust can be traced back to the early days of Nazi Germany. Soon after Adolf Hitler took power, anti-Jewish measures were enacted, including the boycott of Jewish businesses and the seizure of Jewish-owned property. Jews were subjected to public humiliation, barred from schools, and excluded from jobs. For centuries, Jews have faced prejudice and discrimination known as anti-Semitism. But the Nazis took this resentment and hatred to an unprecedented level. After Germany's defeat in World War I, Jewish people in Europe became scapegoats for the economic problems that plagued the continent. Hitler was violently anti-Semitic and believed that Jews were plotting the downfall of Western civilization. Upon his rise to power, he swore to eliminate these *Untermenschen*, people he considered racially inferior to pure, "Aryan" Germanic peoples.

In 1933, Dachau concentration camp was established, initially as a detention facility for political prisoners and opponents of Hitler's regime. These included communists, socialists, Roma, Jehovah's Witnesses, and homosexuals. Throughout the 1930s, the persecution of German Jews intensified, culminating with the violent *Kristallnacht* (the "Night of Broken Glass") in November 1938. Nazi stormtroopers burned Jewish places of worship and destroyed numerous Jewish businesses and homes. Soon after, they began arresting Jewish men, interning them at the Dachau, Buchenwald, and Sachsenhausen concentration camps. When Germany invaded Poland in 1939, death squads known as *Einsatzgruppen*—part of the Waffen-SS, Nazi Germany's elite paramilitary force—were deployed alongside frontline troops. These units were tasked with eliminating the Jewish population of eastern Europe by any means necessary. Most victims were shot and buried in mass graves. The mass killings committed by the *Einsatzgruppen* were the first steps toward genocide and marked the beginning of the Holocaust.

UP FOR DEBATE: FORCED LABOR IN NAZI GERMANY

The Holocaust was one of the most systematic and well-planned genocides in history. It involved nearly every aspect of German society. The murder of six million Jews was carried out with great efficiency. Detailed records were kept on the number of people killed, and looted Jewish valuables were expertly cataloged and stored. Death camps were run like factories, eliminating a designated number of people per day. But because of the resources and manpower required to carry out the Holocaust, it may have actually contributed to the downfall of Nazi Germany. As the war progressed, supplies and personnel used in perpetrating the Holocaust were needed at the front lines. Because the Nazi leadership remained obsessed with eliminating Europe's Jewish population, the Holocaust, it can be argued, hindered the German war effort, diverting much-needed men and materials. In contrast, forced slave labor was instrumental in projects and industries across the Third Reich, including the construction of the Atlantic Wall.

In 1942, in an effort to expedite the elimination of European Jews, top Nazi and Waffen-SS leaders devised "the final solution to the Jewish question." Extermination camps were established where Jews could be transported and systematically eradicated en masse. Millions of "undesirables" were soon moved by rail car to camps across occupied Europe. The Nazis maintained forced labor, internment, and extermination facilities, but the term *concentration camp* is often used to encompass the entire system. The most infamous of the Nazi camps was Auschwitz-Birkenau, a death factory where at least 1.1 million Jews perished, along with 70,000 Poles, 25,000 Roma, and approximately 15,000 prisoners of war. Gas chambers were used to eradicate large numbers of men, women, and children in short periods of time. The bodies of these gassed victims were then burned in massive crematoria. When Allied troops first came across the concentration camps in the spring of 1945, they were appalled by what they saw. In fact, the scene was so disturbing that General Eisenhower gave orders to document the camps to the fullest extent to prove to the world that such an unfathomable atrocity had actually occurred. When the war ended, war crimes trials were held, and the perpetrators of these atrocities were held accountable. Many were sentenced to long prison terms or executed for their crimes.

The Battle of Berlin

By April 1945, the Allies were rapidly advancing into Germany from the west. Meanwhile, the Soviet Union had capitalized on a series of successful offensives throughout 1943 and 1944 and were approaching Berlin from the east. Under constant aerial bombardment from the British and Americans, the citizens of Berlin led difficult lives. Morale was at an all-time low, and only the most fanatical Nazis clung to the false hope of victory. But despite the ferocity of the bombing from the Western Allies, it wasn't the British or the Americans that Berliners feared most. It was the Soviets.

Since the beginning of his political career, Hitler was a staunch anti-communist. In his fiery speeches he preached hateful rhetoric about far-left politics. This propaganda onslaught successfully developed a nearly universal hatred and fear of the Soviet Union among the German population. So when the residents of Berlin began to realize that the war was lost and the mighty Red Army was on its way, panic and terror ensued. Many frightened residents fled the city and headed west toward the advancing Allied armies. Others stayed to await their fate. Although much of Germany's fear of communism and the Soviet Union was based upon unfounded claims, the Red Army did have a strong sense of vengeance. The Germans had waged a war of unimaginable brutality on the Eastern Front, and the people of the Soviet Union had experienced terrible suffering and deprivation. The Soviets were determined to make the Germans pay. And after several years of bitter conflict, the tide had turned. The Soviet Union was prepared to wipe the Third Reich from the map.

With the Soviets rapidly advancing, Nazi propaganda minister Joseph Goebbels mustered a civilian force to assist in the defense of the city. Known as the *Volkssturm*, or People's Militia, this ragtag army was mainly comprised of women and old men, many of them veterans of World War I. Most were issued no uniforms and commonly wore civilian clothes with an attached red and black armband that read: *Deutscher Volkssturm Wehrmacht* ("German People's Militia Army"). They were often armed with antiquated weapons and issued just a few rounds of ammunition. Others were given more serious weaponry, such as the *Panzerfaust*, an inexpensive, single-shot anti-tank weapon that required little training. Serving alongside the Volkssturm were the Hitler-Jugend (Hitler Youth) and Bund Deutscher Mädel (League of German Girls). These were the youth paramilitary organizations of the Nazi Party. The Hitler Youth was created in 1933 and served to indoctrinate and train male youth into becoming ideal Nazis. The League of German Girls was the female wing of the youth movement and served a similar purpose. When the Battle of Berlin began, thousands of boys and girls as young as 14 years

SOVIET TROOPS IN THE STREETS OF BERLIN, 1945

old were sent out into the streets to operate machine guns, *Panzerfausts*, and even artillery.

For the Soviets, the capture of Berlin was the ultimate prize, and with the Allies quickly approaching from the west, Red Army commanders sought a way to reach the city first. They developed a plan to encircle Berlin before beginning their assault. The tactic would keep the British and Americans out and besiege the German defenders inside. On April 16, 1945, fighting began at Seelow Heights, on the outskirts of the city. A massive Soviet army of almost one million soldiers and 20,000 tanks and artillery pieces was deployed, and by April 20, Berlin was completely surrounded. The city was then subjected to a massive Soviet artillery barrage, reducing much of the Nazi capital to rubble. Five days later, on April 25, Red Army troops were in Berlin itself and were met with stubborn resistance from the German defenders. Just as in Stalingrad, fierce urban warfare commenced across the city as the Germans fought for every block, street, and house. The Soviets expended many men and great quantities of resources to gain a foothold in the city. Red Army tanks took heavy losses to *Panzerfausts*, while the infantry were subjected to machine-gun fire and snipers positioned atop the buildings. Soviet Katyusha rocket launchers were used in large numbers, and their sight and terrifying sound became a symbol of the Battle for Berlin.

Throughout the battle, Hitler was holed up in a massive underground bunker complex (or "Führerbunker") beneath the Reichstag, Nazi Germany's ceremonial parliament building. Inside his bunker, Hitler and the last followers of the Nazi regime could hear the Soviet artillery as it drew closer each day. Despite reports from his generals, Hitler refused to believe the war was lost and remained committed to the idea that Berlin would rise from the ashes. He grew delusional with his commands, giving orders to units and divisions that no longer existed. By April 30, the Red Army had occupied most of Berlin and was nearing the Reichstag. As Soviet forces approached his bunker, Hitler married his longtime girlfriend, Eva Braun, and the two committed suicide. Within days, Red Army troops breached the Reichstag in fierce close-quarters combat and raised the Soviet flag atop the once infamous symbol of Nazi power. Berlin had fallen.

When Hitler first took power in 1933, he boasted that the Third Reich would last for 1,000 years. His perverted dreams of world domination and Germanic supremacy came to a crashing end after just 12 years. The days of Nazi Germany were over.

CHAPTER 7

THE FINAL THROES OF WAR IN THE PACIFIC

In 1945, Japan was still an imminent threat. But the United States was bound and determined to bring that threat to an end. The Japanese were prepared to defend every inch of territory leading up to their homeland and fought with fierce determination as the Americans drew closer by the day. The final throes of war in the Pacific would prove to be the deadliest of them all, introducing new kinds of warfare, wiping entire cities from the map, and sending thousands of young American soldiers home in flag-draped coffins.

To the Mainland

Victory over Nazi Germany was met with great relief to those back home and celebrated by servicemen and -women overseas in Europe. But for the soldiers, sailors, marines, and airmen who were fighting in the Pacific, the European victory had little effect. There was still a lot of ground to be covered before the Japanese could be forced into submission. After recapturing the Philippines, the road to Japan appeared open. But the worst battles were yet to come. The Pacific island-hopping campaign had already resulted in many casualties, and the brutal jungle combat was exhausting. American soldiers were unfamiliar with this style of warfare, while the Japanese had been preparing for it for years. Disease was prevalent, and many American troops fell ill to malaria, typhus, or just plain combat fatigue.

American naval and air forces had unquestionable superiority on the sea and in the skies. Despite this, the Japanese maintained strong resistance, defending every speck of land that led to their home islands. Suicide attacks, known as banzai charges, took place in almost every campaign but were used in greater numbers as the Japanese started to run out of ammunition and firearms. American soldiers were often faced with thousands of screaming Japanese troops rushing toward them, armed with only bayonets or samurai swords. It was a terrifying experience for the Americans and incredibly foolish for, and brave of, the Japanese, who were instantly mowed down by heavy gunfire. The enemy did not abide by the "rules of war": They rarely took prisoners and often targeted American medics, because they knew that more soldiers would die without medical assistance. This made the Pacific campaign unusually savage. Under great duress in combat situations, this Japanese savagery was often matched by the Americans. In mainstream U.S. newspapers and government-produced propaganda, the Japanese were often called degrading racial slurs.

But the level of hatred toward the Japanese went far beyond racially motivated insults. In early 1942, after the Japanese attack on Pearl Harbor, President Franklin D. Roosevelt signed Executive Order 9066. This law called for all Japanese Americans to be rounded up and interned at detention facilities for the duration of the war. Fears of espionage, sabotage, and anti-American activity served as the motivation for this now-infamous decision. All across the country, more than 120,000 people of Japanese ancestry, some 80,000 of them American citizens, were forced to abruptly leave their homes, sell their possessions, and relocate to internment camps. They were interned without due process or formal charges and transported into captivity solely based on their race and national origin. These drastic measures are a true testament to the fear and anger that Americans felt. They are also evidence of the institutional racism that plagued 1940s America. Many Americans did not even consider the Japanese to be human. Unlike in Europe, where there was some sense of respect between enemies, the Pacific war was an all-out fight to the death. There was no human aspect.

The Manhattan Project

Throughout the 1930s, German scientists were working to harness the power of atomic energy to make a bomb. The state-sponsored research program gathered scientific minds from across the country to research and develop a nuclear weapon for the Third Reich. By 1939, the Germans had learned the secrets of splitting a uranium atom and were making rapid progress on their research. This troubled the world scientific community, who recognized the danger of a nuclear weapon in the hands of Adolf Hitler.

But several of Germany's top scientists and atomic physicists were Jewish. And with the rise of Nazism, they fled the nation. One of them was Albert Einstein, a physicist, who came to the United States in 1933. Einstein was well aware of the Nazi nuclear program and became an early advocate for the creation of a rival American program. He penned a letter to President Roosevelt urging him to invest in atomic research. Although Roosevelt was not too keen on the idea, Einstein persuaded him to create the Manhattan Project. This was a research group that would eventually produce the first nuclear bomb. The program was initially confined to research at universities. But when World War II erupted, the Manhattan Project was given as much funding and resources as it needed.

MANHATTAN PROJECT PHYSICISTS AT LOS ALAMOS, NEW MEXICO, 1940S

Under the leadership of physicist J. Robert Oppenheimer, the secret nationwide effort harnessed the skills of thousands of scientists, engineers, and soldiers at research and testing facilities. The Los Alamos National Laboratory in New Mexico was at the forefront of the project, eventually becoming the site of the first nuclear explosion in history. Roosevelt was kept informed about the top secret work, but even his vice president, Harry S. Truman, was unaware of the groundbreaking research. When Roosevelt died on April 12, 1945, Harry Truman became president of the United States. Truman was promptly briefed about the nation's efforts to develop atomic weapons. At this stage in the war, Manhattan Project scientists had successfully created and tested an atomic weapon in the deserts of New Mexico. But by the time their research and development was complete, Germany had already surrendered, and the threat from the Nazi nuclear program eliminated. In the meantime, U.S. troops were facing heavy casualties in the Pacific theater, where they were fighting a long and bloody campaign toward the Japanese archipelago.

The Battle of Iwo Jima

By late 1944, American forces had advanced into Japan's outer islands and were rapidly pushing toward the main islands. Following the capture of the Mariana Islands, American military leaders determined that the next target would be the island of Iwo Jima, located 750 miles off the coast of Japan. Its capture would provide American Boeing B-29 bombers with emergency landing strips when returning from raids. Iwo Jima could also be used as a staging area for the anticipated invasion of the Japanese main islands. Due to the weakened state of the Japanese navy and air force, American planners believed the battle would last just a few days and incur minimal casualties. In February 1945, American naval and air

forces began the invasion with a massive three-day bombardment of the island. It was reported that not a single tree was
left standing.

**FIVE U.S. MARINES AND A U.S. NAVY CORPSMAN RAISE A
U.S. FLAG DURING THE BATTLE OF IWO JIMA, FEBRUARY 1945**

When the first marines approached the shore on February
19, they met little resistance. The landing force figured that
the massive bombing had killed all of the Japanese defenders.
But the Japanese garrison had not been eliminated. In fact,
they had escaped the bombing almost entirely unscathed. In
the years leading up to the battle, Japanese soldiers stationed
on Iwo Jima had constructed an elaborate system of passage-
ways inside the volcanic terrain. They erected fortifications of

every shape and size, from artillery bunkers in the mountains to machine-gun nests on the coast. Despite being outnumbered, the Japanese were incredibly resourceful. When the American barrage began, they hunkered down inside their tunnels and caves and waited for the amphibious assault to begin. The Japanese watched as the first wave of U.S. Marines disembarked their landing craft onto the black volcanic sands. They waited for hundreds of troops to come ashore before opening fire, inflicting the maximum number of casualties. Japanese cannons opened fire from their emplacements, while machine guns located in camouflaged bunkers tore into the marines pinned down on the beach. As the exposed troops struggled to crawl inland, the Japanese made them pay for every inch of ground, displaying fanatical resistance. Both sides suffered thousands of casualties.

Eventually, the landing force was reorganized and reinforcements arrived. The marines knocked out the enemy positions that threatened the beachhead. Japanese soldiers were flushed from their caves by flamethrowers and automatic weapons, and the American troops began the long journey inland. On the fourth day of the battle, with combat still raging across the island, a group of marines ascended the slopes of Mount Suribachi and raised the American flag at the peak of the 554-foot extinct volcano. This would become one of World War II's most iconic images, motivating the weary troops and inspiring the Americans back home. Joe Rosenthal's photograph became a symbol of American triumph in the Pacific theater. The image was published in newspapers and magazines across the country, used on war bond and recruitment posters, and made celebrities out of the flag raisers themselves. The battle for Iwo Jima dragged on for several more weeks, but the photograph had sparked a new wave of patriotism and national pride, reinvigorating the war effort.

By March 3, U.S. forces had secured the airfields on the island, and on March 26, Iwo Jima was declared secure. The entire Japanese garrison had been wiped out; only 216 of the 18,000 defenders were captured alive. Of the 70,000 U.S. marines who fought to take Iwo Jima, almost 7,000 lost their lives; it was one of the U.S. Marine Corps' costliest battles of World War II. The brutal fighting proved that Japan was not prepared to surrender and that their defense would grow increasingly defiant as the Americans approached the main islands. The heavy casualties sustained on Iwo Jima were of great concern to U.S. military leaders, who recognized that the worst was yet to come.

A MATTER OF CHOICE: THE PRICE PAID ON IWO JIMA

Iwo Jima was chosen as a target on the path to Japan because it was believed that the island's airstrips could be used as a base for B-29 bombers. Plus, it would provide returning aircraft with safe emergency landing strips. American military leaders thought they could keep the losses of landing troops to a minimum by destroying most of the Japanese garrison by air and sea bombardment. As history has shown, this turned out to be a fatal assumption. Once the island was secured, Navy Seabees ("CBs," for *construction battalions*) were successful in rebuilding Iwo Jima's two airfields and constructing a third. But the value of these air bases was soon questioned. Crippled aircraft did make many emergency landings on the island instead of being forced into the sea, saving the lives of countless airmen. But when the public became aware of the immense sacrifice made to capture the island, many felt the benefits did not exceed the enormous losses, raising the central question: Was Iwo Jima worth the cost?

Strategic Bombing

As the Americans drew closer to the Japanese home islands, their aircraft were now in range of Japan's largest cities. The Army Air Forces were then prompted to initiate a "strategic bombing" campaign with the intent of crippling the enemy's war industry and the morale of its citizens. Beginning in June of 1944, large formations of American bombers carried out daytime attacks. They targeted factories, rail yards, and other areas of manufacturing, production, and transportation. The most common aircraft used in these raids was the Boeing B-29 Superfortress, a heavy bomber that boasted innovative technology and long-range capabilities. But the daytime attacks yielded minimal results. The B-29s soon switched to night raids, this time targeting civilians. The motive of these attacks was to destroy the will of the Japanese people to continue to fight in the hope that the government would sue for peace. But as the months went on and civilian casualties began to mount, the Japanese continued to refuse to negotiate with the Allies. The bombing continued.

On the night of March 9–10, 1945, American B-29s set out to bomb Tokyo, Japan's capital. This would become the single-most destructive bombing raid in history. The aircraft were armed with bombs specially designed to induce fires upon impact. Over the course of a few hours, more than 2,000 tons of bombs were dropped in and around Tokyo, razing the entire city to the ground. The bombing focused on the old area of central Tokyo known as *shitamachi*. More than 750,000 civilian residents lived there in close quarters in wooden buildings. At the time, Tokyo had one of the highest population densities of any city in the world. The homes were engulfed in flames within a matter of seconds as the fires spread rapidly. Japanese fire departments lacked the technology or experience to extinguish the fires and were forced to watch their city burn. The firebombing of Tokyo left more than 100,000 civilians dead and close to one million homeless. There has been a long-running debate regarding the morality and necessity of these attacks that inflicted heavy losses on targets of little to no military importance. Some even call it a war crime. The destruction and devastation was unimaginable. Yet, Japan's military and government still refused to end the suffering, carrying on the fight even after it was clear the war was lost.

ARMS AND ARMOR: THE B-29 SUPERFORTRESS BOMBER

If there's one aircraft synonymous with the Pacific theater, it's the B-29 Superfortress. The versatile and technologically advanced bomber dominated the skies over Japan in World War II. Manufactured by Boeing, the B-29 weighed 105,000 pounds and could fly at speeds of up to 365 miles per hour. Its ten-man crew operated an ultramodern 99-foot-long aircraft that had an extended flying range, radio-controlled guns, and pressurized cabins. The plane was designed for high-altitude bombing, but many were also used with great success in low-altitude incendiary raids over Tokyo and other Japanese cities. B-29s were also used to drop atomic bombs, on both Hiroshima and Nagasaki, and remained a prominent part of the United States Air Force (established in 1947 as a separate branch of the U.S. armed forces) for years to come.

The Battle of Okinawa

The island of Okinawa was the last stop on America's island-hopping campaign toward the Japanese mainland. It was a large and highly-populated stretch of land situated just 400 miles from Kyushu, the southernmost main island of Japan. The island offered large air bases and docking facilities for ships, making it the perfect staging point for an amphibious assault. American planners sought to capture Okinawa as a base for a possible Allied invasion of Japan. Code-named Operation Iceberg, the invasion of Okinawa was a joint operation between the U.S. Army, Navy, and Marine Corps. Land forces were commanded by Lieutenant General Simon Bolivar Buckner Jr., who led three Marine and four Army divisions into combat. Offshore, Admiral Raymond Spruance commanded the U.S. Fifth Fleet that constituted more than 1,300 warships and landing craft. In late March 1945, U.S. Navy ships began a weeklong bombardment to soften up the island's defenses. As on Iwo Jima, the Japanese defenders had built an elaborate system of interconnected tunnels and caves. Consequently, the naval bombardment had little effect. The Japanese soldiers escaped the bombing with few casualties and prepared for the oncoming assault.

At this point in the war, the Japanese had developed a solid plan to defend against American amphibious invasions, even if only to inflict maximum casualties without hope of victory. General Mitsuru Ushijima, commander of the Japanese garrison on Okinawa, had spread his forces across a series of defensive lines. Instead of holding the entire island, Ushijima fortified certain strategic areas where the terrain was ideal for entrenched positions and tactical ambushes. The Americans were superior in numbers and maintained complete air supremacy, but the Japanese defenders were prepared to hold the island to the last man. On April 1, 1945, the first American troops came ashore at Okinawa. Encountering no resistance, the landing was eerily reminiscent of the campaign on Iwo Jima a few months prior. The situation remained quiet for the rest of the day, and by dusk, 50,000 American troops had made it ashore. After an uneventful landing, the marines moved to the north, while the Army traveled south, fighting toward the key strongpoints on each end of the island.

Meanwhile at sea, the Japanese launched Operation Ten-Go. They sent their super-battleship *Yamato* and several other smaller warships to disrupt the American landings. Their effort was thwarted, however, when U.S. Navy submarines and aircraft located the Japanese fleet. Massive air strikes sank the *Yamato* and her escort vessels. Japanese kamikaze pilots were also used in large numbers during the fierce air and sea battle. By the end, the Japanese had launched almost 2,000 suicide attacks against American ships, and close to 5,000 sailors were killed as a result. Back on land, the marines were overcoming the Japanese defenses in the north, but opposition to the south proved formidable. Heavy rains and rugged terrain hindered the American advance. In addition, camouflaged Japanese positions constantly harassed and ambushed the attacking troops. The heart of the Japanese defense was based at the historic Shuri Castle, which was surrounded by well-defended high cliffs. Ushijima's forces maintained a vigorous defense, inflicting heavy losses on the bogged-down American troops. Shuri Castle finally fell on May 29, and the marines were able to continue their advance across the island. On June 4, a second amphibious assault was launched, leading to the capture of the strategic airfield at Naha. The Battle for Okinawa would last nearly three months, the longest of any Pacific campaign. By July 2, 1945, the island was declared secure, and American forces began to come ashore en masse in preparation for the assault on the Japanese mainland.

The battle was ultimately an American victory, but it came at a heavy cost. The unexpectedly high casualties on Okinawa was a huge wake-up call for American military leaders. It proved how ferocious the Japanese would be as the marines drew closer to their homeland. The battle of Okinawa was the largest and deadliest Pacific campaign, claiming the lives of some 12,500 Americans—including General Buckner—and wounding at least 35,000 more. Approximately 110,000 Japanese soldiers were killed in action, nearly the entire garrison that defended the island. Brainwashed into thinking that the Americans would commit mass rape and murder, Japanese civilians in the thousands committed suicide by jumping from Okinawa's steep cliffs. It is estimated that total civilian deaths numbered as many as 150,000. Nonetheless, victory on Okinawa put Allied forces within striking distance of the main islands of Japan, a nation prepared to defend their homeland to the last man, woman, and child.

Hiroshima and Nagasaki

After the slaughters on Iwo Jima and Okinawa, American military planners were distraught by the idea of an amphibious landing on mainland Japan. Their predictions estimated that American casualties would number up to 4 million, while Japanese casualties might be as high as 19 million. To avoid such bloodshed, they proposed using nuclear weapons on Japanese cities to hasten the end of the war and save the lives of countless American troops. In July of 1945, Manhattan Project scientists detonated the world's first atomic bomb in the desert of New Mexico. Their success gave the military leaders the alternative strategy they were searching for. With the fate of so many young soldiers resting in the balance, President Harry Truman made the fateful decision to unleash the first of two atomic bombs on Japan. The cataclysmic events that followed would bring the Manhattan Project and nuclear energy to the forefront of world debate and criticism.

ATOMIC BOMBING OF NAGASAKI, AUGUST 9, 1945

It was a calm and sunny morning on August 6, 1945, when the B-29 bomber *Enola Gay* departed the American air base on the island of Tinian. Its destination: the city of Hiroshima. At approximately 8:15 a.m. local time, the bomb, nicknamed "Little Boy," was dropped on the city. The explosion was equal to 15 kilotons of TNT, and it sent a radioactive blast wave across the densely populated metropolis. Almost immediately, five square miles of Hiroshima were reduced to ashes, turning the city into a toxic wasteland. An enormous mushroom cloud of smoke and debris rose above the ruins of a once-proud and prosperous city. Hiroshima was chosen as the first target of an atomic bomb due to its economic and military significance to the Japanese war effort. But the destruction also took an unfathomable toll on the civilian population. It is estimated that 70,000 people were immediately vaporized by the blast, and within four days more than 120,000 had perished, with a five-year death toll of as high as 200,000. Those who were lucky enough to survive would never be the same. They would suffer from severe radiation poisoning and other medical ailments all their lives.

The initial response from the Japanese government was silence. They were not sure what to believe of reports that claimed an entire city was devastated by one bomb. Today there is considerable knowledge about nuclear weapons and their impact, but in 1945 this weapon was entirely new to the world. Understandably, the Japanese had doubts about the accounts of mass destruction. But three days later, with the Japanese surrender still not forthcoming, the Americans chose a second target. On August 9, another B-29 from the Tinian air base dropped an atomic bomb on Nagasaki, a large coastal city on the Japanese island of Kyushu. This bomb was nicknamed "Fat Man"; it had the explosive force of 21 kilotons of TNT and produced devastating results similar to those of the Hiroshima bomb. Three square miles of the city were leveled, with a total of 43 square miles affected, and approximately 40,000 people were killed immediately, with another 30,000 deaths by January 1946. Even after this second bombing and catastrophic destruction, it took the Japanese government another week to finally accept defeat. Military hard-liners sought to continue the war even after Hiroshima and Nagasaki. They agreed to surrender only after a strong intervention from Emperor Hirohito himself.

The atomic bombs ended World War II without the loss of any additional American troops. But victory came at a terrible cost to the Japanese civilian population. Before the bombings, no one truly understood the impact a nuclear weapon could have on human lives. All tests had been conducted on nonliving targets. The destruction the weapons caused appalled even the scientists who had created the bombs and sent shockwaves across the world. This new kind of warfare would define the rest of the 20th century, sparking a nuclear arms race between the United States and the Soviet Union at the height of the Cold War.

UP FOR DEBATE: THE ATOMIC BOMB

Since the end of World War II, there has been widespread debate regarding the ethical and moral justifications of the atomic bombing of Hiroshima and Nagasaki. American military leaders firmly believed their decision prevented huge numbers of casualties and avoided a costly invasion of mainland Japan. Immediately after the war, a vast majority of Americans supported the decision. Yet, over time, public opinion has shifted. According to a survey conducted by the Pew Research Center in 2015, only 56 percent of Americans believe the bombings were justified. Little Boy and Fat Man undoubtedly brought about a more rapid victory and spared the lives of countless American troops. But the civilian losses caused by the bombs certainly raise valid moral questions about their use. The first and only use of nuclear weapons in combat remains one of World War II's most controversial topics and is a widely debated issue across the globe.

CHAPTER 8

AFTERMATH AND IMPACT

The year 1945 brought about the collapse of both Nazi Germany and Imperial Japan. The surrender of the Axis powers not only returned peace to the world but also marked the beginning of new challenges for the global community. Divided between two radically different political ideologies and facing a disastrous economic crisis, Europe was on the brink of collapse. At the same time, the Japanese worked diligently to rebuild the ruins of their nation. The postwar years proved a tumultuous time as the world struggled to recover from the most destructive war in human history.

The End of the War in Europe

After the fall of Berlin and Adolf Hitler's suicide in April 1945, it was clear that the Third Reich had collapsed. In Hitler's final will and testament, he appointed Grand Admiral Karl Dönitz as his successor. Negotiations began immediately with the Soviets and the Western Allies. Dönitz and the German high command sought a negotiated peace, but the victors demanded unconditional surrender. Shortly after midnight Berlin time on May 8, 1945, Field Marshal Wilhelm Keitel signed the surrender documents on behalf of the German government. Present were dozens of Allied officers, including Soviet marshal Georgy Zhukov, who had led the assault on Berlin from the east. Keitel's reluctant signature ended five years, eight months, and seven days of war in Europe. Even after the surrender, scattered fighting continued across Germany as the last pockets of resistance were flushed out or learned of their country's capitulation. When Berlin was captured, more than three million German prisoners of war fell into Soviet hands. Those lucky enough to survive the perilous journey eastward to Siberia were subjected to harsh treatment in internment camps. The POWs were forced to endure hard labor and freezing temperatures. It wasn't until 1956, eleven years after the end of the war, that the last German POW was released from Soviet captivity. Close to 400,000 never returned.

Postwar Germany was divided into four sectors, each controlled by one of the leading Allied powers. The Soviet Union retained control of the eastern half, while the United States, Great Britain, and France occupied sectors in the west. Berlin was split down the middle—the western half under Allied occupation and the Soviets with control of the eastern half. The Soviet occupation of Berlin was especially brutal. Thousands of women of all ages were raped and murdered by Red Army soldiers. German citizens and soldiers alike feared the Soviet occupiers, and many migrated westward toward the Allied lines. In 1949, the western zone became the Federal Republic of Germany, commonly known as West Germany. The eastern sector was inaugurated as the German Democratic Republic, or East Germany. The latter was strongly influenced by the Soviet Union, while West Germany maintained a more independent government. The occupation of Germany in 1945 resulted in a divided nation that became a hot spot of the ideological struggle between capitalism and communism. The reunification of Germany did not occur until the fall of the Berlin Wall in 1989 and the dissolution of the Soviet Union in 1991.

World War II had lasting repercussions for the entire European continent and continues to be a relevant aspect of society today. Much of Europe's modern political structure can even be traced back to the war. The European Union, a collective group of 27 nations that are united economically and politically, was created after World War II. Its aim is to end future conflicts between neighboring countries. Unlike the failed League of Nations, the EU has proven to be effective, preserving peace and stability in Europe. Furthermore, more than 75 years after the war, large commemorations take place to honor and remember the men and women who fought and died to free Europe from the Third Reich. And although the Soviet Union no longer exists, Russian remembrance of the Great Patriotic War is an integral part of their culture. Despite the massive losses suffered by the Soviets, they emerged from World War II as a world power, making the early postwar years a proud time in Soviet (and Russian) history. Each year on the anniversary of Germany's surrender, a parade is held in Moscow honoring the Red Army's sacrifices and paying tribute to the Soviet victory over fascism. Most European nations made a remarkable recovery following the destruction and devastation of World War II. And although the war seems so far in the past, its impact on the Europe we know today is more noticeable now than ever.

The End of the War in the Pacific

The Pacific War would continue for more than three months following victory in Europe, its climax coming with the atomic bombing of Hiroshima and Nagasaki in August of 1945. These attacks came as a great shock to Japan, and many military officers still sought to continue the war against the United States. When Emperor Hirohito proposed negotiations with the Allies, military hard-liners attempted a coup against the government. Their efforts were in vain. On August 15, in a radio broadcast to his empire, Hirohito announced Japan's unconditional surrender. In his somber speech, he noted that the use of "a new and most cruel bomb" had led to the surrender and that further fighting would only cause "an ultimate collapse and obliteration of the Japanese nation."

JAPANESE OFFICERS SURRENDER THEIR SWORDS TO BRITISH SOLDIERS AT THE END OF WORLD WAR II, 1945

For most Japanese civilians, this was the first time they had ever heard their leader's voice. On September 2, 1945, a Japanese delegation boarded the American battleship USS *Missouri* in Tokyo Bay and signed the Japanese Instrument of Surrender, the documents that formally ended World War II. In the presence of hundreds of Allied officers, Foreign Minister Mamoru Shigemitsu and General Yoshijiro Umezu signed their names and brought peace to the Pacific. Japan's surrender saved the lives of hundreds of thousands of Americans as well as Japanese soldiers and civilians.

News of Japan's capitulation spread like wildfire. Thousands filled the streets of American cities, celebrating the victory and the restoration of peace in the world. Following Japan's unconditional surrender, President Harry Truman appointed General Douglas MacArthur to lead the occupation. MacArthur was given the daunting task of restoring Japan's economy, rebuilding its infrastructure, and dismantling its military. From 1945 to 1952, the Americans instituted numerous political, economic, and social reforms in Japan. Miles of new roads and railways, previously destroyed by Allied bombs, were replaced. Factories were reconstructed, and production was started from the ground up. U.S. occupation forces also controlled most aspects of the government. But as a token of respect to Japanese culture, Emperor Hirohito was kept in power as a ceremonial figure. The Japanese viewed their emperor as a godlike leader, and stripping them of that god would have caused untold fear and panic across the country. The controversial decision to keep Hirohito in power served to appease the Japanese population and prove that America was not out to destroy their culture and national identity.

The postwar Japanese constitution renounced war and vowed to never again use force as a means to solve a dispute. To this day, Japan is not permitted to maintain a formal military with offensive capabilities. Instead, it relies on a large domestic security apparatus known as the Japan Self-Defense Forces. As the power that forced Japan to disband its armed forces, the United States still maintains a sizable military presence in the Pacific, including a large base on Okinawa. Since World War II ended in 1945, American military forces have assisted the Japanese with their national defense. In recent years, Japan and the United States have become close allies, working together to combat rising aggression on the part of China and North Korea.

The Push to Rebuild

Japan's surrender marked the beginning of a new era, one defined by atomic energy, the struggle between communism and capitalism, and the United States' emergence as a world superpower. But when World War II ended in Europe, America didn't just pack up and go home. Immediately following Germany's surrender, an elaborate denazification program was instituted by the Allied military government. Its purpose was to remove all aspects of the Nazi regime from postwar German society. Civilians from all walks of life went through mandatory rehabilitation to learn about the crimes of Nazi Germany and be reeducated with democratic values. On a larger scale, targets of denazification efforts included the court system and the press, as well as federal, state, and local governments. The Allies not only worked to eradicate all traces of Nazism in postwar German life; they also sought to bring the perpetrators of Nazi war crimes to justice. National socialist ideas were banned and deemed punishable by death. And many top-ranking Nazis were brought to trial to answer for their crimes. In late 1945, the Nuremberg war crimes trials were held in Germany. The surviving Nazi leaders, including Hermann Göring, Wilhelm Keitel, and Albert Speer, faced a military tribunal and were held accountable for their wartime actions. Most were sentenced to long prison terms or death by hanging. Similar trials were held in Japan, where government and military leaders were sentenced for war crimes and crimes against humanity.

THE NUREMBERG TRIALS, GERMANY, NOVEMBER 1945–OCTOBER 1946

The U.S. government recognized that most German and Japanese civilians did not support or condone the war, and these populations were now left with crippled nations, destroyed economies, and uncertain futures. In response, America spent billions of dollars to transform the postwar lives of their former enemies, ensuring that the citizens of the now-occupied nations recovered from the destruction. Europe had been subjected to massive bombardments from Allied aircraft, leaving its cities in ruins. As an answer to these problems, the U.S. government devised an aid program to support western European infrastructure and rebuilding efforts. Known as the Marshall Plan, this reconstruction program cost the United States close to $15 billion over a period of four years. It provided aid and funding to several European countries to assist in economic development.

NEWSPAPER ARTICLE OUTLINING THE DETAILS OF THE MARSHALL PLAN, 1947

The money was given as a grant, and the countries that received funds were not required to repay the United States. The Marshall Plan, also known as the European Recovery Program, was the brainchild of American General George C. Marshall. He was an early advocate for "good deed foreign policy" to rebuild the ruins of western Europe in the wake of World War II. Marshall's vision finally came to reality in 1948 and provided much-needed assistance to 17 nations: West Germany, Great Britain, France, Italy, the Netherlands, Ireland, Norway, Austria, Belgium, Denmark, Greece, Iceland, Luxembourg, Sweden, Portugal, Switzerland, and Turkey.

Although the plan was pitched solely as a humanitarian effort, there were numerous political motivations. The Marshall Plan showed that the United States sought to maintain its influence in western Europe in the face of rising tensions with the Soviet Union. The U.S. government was also concerned about the weakened economies of several European nations, fearing they would fall prey to communism. To avoid antagonizing the Soviets, Marshall offered aid to eastern European countries under Russian control. Most of these countries declined under pressure from Moscow. Joseph Stalin was working to build the Soviet Union's image as a world power and a self-sufficient nation. He feared that accepting the Marshall Plan aid would weaken his rule and allow capitalism to influence his communist regime. In the end, the countries that did benefit from the plan experienced significant economic growth and reinvigorated industries. The Marshall Plan was widely successful in rebuilding European nations and ensured the continent's stability in the postwar years.

LEGACY

lthough the United States was racially divided in the 1940s and the military was segregated, America's cultural melting pot became the backbone of the efforts against the Axis powers. Segregated units like the all-black Tuskegee Airmen and the Japanese American Nisei soldiers endured racial discrimination that knew no bounds. Yet, these soldiers went on to become war heroes. Indigenous code talkers used their languages to help secure victory in some of the Pacific War's most crucial battles. At a time when it was difficult for America's diverse population to find success back home, they embraced their wartime roles and became some of the most decorated units of World War II. Moreover, American women embraced traditionally male roles on the home front, while others stood shoulder to shoulder with their male counterparts in the military.

America's World War II veterans—now widely known as the "Greatest Generation"—returned home to build the country we know today. These servicemen and -women had children and began to raise families. The resulting growth in the population became known as the baby boom. Compared to other nations, the United States thrived in the years following World War II. The country became a world superpower and an international symbol of freedom and democracy. Since then, the United States has worked hard to protect the liberties that young soldiers fought and died to preserve on battlefields across Europe and the Pacific. The freedom from fear and want and the freedoms of speech and religion are the core values for which so many men and women made the ultimate sacrifice.

As you reflect on the content presented in this book, I hope you will understand the three-dimensional way in which World War II was covered, beginning with the prelude to the conflict; the war itself; and, lastly, the enormous impact the war has had on society. Today's global nuclear capabilities and computerized warfare almost ensure that the world will never have another war like World War II. A future global conflict could easily result in the collapse and destruction of the entire planet and human civilization. We must always strive to preserve peace at all costs, as the price of war is greater than any of us can ever imagine.

As we move forward with our lives in this ultramodern world, it is essential not to lose sight of what has occurred in our past and how it brought us to the present day. Undoubtedly we will face numerous challenges in the future. But we must always remember that, as a united society, we can persevere. According to a quote widely attributed to renowned writer Mark Twain, "History doesn't repeat itself, but it often rhymes," subtly indicating how events in our past tend to reoccur. As the next generation of world leaders, it is your responsibility and sacred duty to remember the past and build a safe and prosperous future. Studying history can help us face our problems as a united society, just as our ancestors did during World War II. By learning the lessons of the past, we can build a better tomorrow and avoid repeating the horrible tragedies that enveloped the world in the first half of the 20th century. The legacy left by the greatest conflict known to mankind is still visible today and more important than ever to understand.

RESOURCES

MUSEUMS

The National WWII Museum

This first-class museum is one of the world's premier historical destinations and features interactive exhibits that are both educational and entertaining. In addition to their impressive New Orleans facility, the National WWII Museum website contains a plethora of information pertaining to the study of the war and its impact on our society. Learn more at NationalWW2Museum.org.

United States Holocaust Memorial Museum

Located in the heart of Washington, DC, the United States Holocaust Memorial Museum is America's official memorial to the Holocaust. The museum maintains a collection of millions of artifacts documenting Nazi Germany and its extensive crimes against humanity during World War II. Much of their vast archive is digitized online and presented in an easy-to-access format. Visit ushmm.org to explore the collection and plan your visit to the museum.

WEBSITES

Library of Congress
The Library of Congress is the national library of the United States and preserves millions of books, recordings, photographs, newspapers, and manuscripts in its collections. Many of its files, including an extensive archive of World War II photographs and documents, are available online. The Library of Congress Veterans History Project is also a fantastic resource to hear directly from veterans about their wartime experiences. For more information, visit LoC.gov.

National Archives and Records Administration
This independent agency of the United States government preserves our nation's history through archival documents, including the records of World War II service members. In recent years, efforts have been made to digitize large amounts of records, but most remain in original paper form at facilities across America. Explore the digitized archive and begin your research into the history of the war at Archives.gov.

WWII Veterans History Project
This Florida-based nonprofit organization is home to an extensive collection of oral histories and historic artifacts, preserving the memories of thousands of World War II veterans for future generations. The WWII Veterans History Project operates a traveling museum of World War II artifacts and maintains one of the world's last surviving Higgins boat landing craft. Interactive presentations for students and inspiring documentary films featuring untold stories are the highlight of this notable institution. Learn more about the nonprofit and its essential work at WW2VeteransHistoryProject.com.

MEDIA

World War II Day by Day by Antony Shaw (2000)

This book provides readers with a unique glimpse at World War II through a chronological perspective, giving a day-by-day timeline from the invasion of Poland to the surrender of Japan. *World War II Day by Day* does an excellent job not only portraying the battles of the conflict but also exploring key figures, the home front, politics, technology, and more.

World War II in HD Colour (2009)

This compelling documentary series tells the story of World War II through remarkable colorized footage and state-of-the-art maps and graphics. Narrated by Robert Powell, *World War II in HD Colour* is among my most highly recommended shows for beginners to immerse themselves in the complicated study of World War II. Although it is an excellent introductory show, the attention to detail and quality of the series is impressive to even the most seasoned history buffs. (It is not to be confused with the 2019 series *Greatest Events of WWII in Colour*.)

The History Channel

While much of the History Channel's television programming has shifted away from World War II in recent years, their website remains a valuable resource for those interested in learning about the war in an unbiased form. Learn more at History.com.

BOOKS

Band of Brothers by Stephen E. Ambrose (1992)

Stephen E. Ambrose's iconic *New York Times* best seller explores World War II through the eyes of Easy Company, 506th Parachute Infantry Regiment, 101st Airborne Division, as they fight across the European continent from France to Austria. Based on interviews with survivors of the unit, this book illustrates the lives of ordinary men who lived through extraordinary times. This masterfully written account was later adapted into an HBO miniseries, *Band of Brothers* (2001). The book and television adaption are must-haves for any World War II buff.

The Diary of a Young Girl by Anne Frank (1947)

Among one of the most revered memoirs of World War II, *The Diary of a Young Girl* is a tragic firsthand account of the Holocaust, written by Jewish teenager Anne Frank as she hid from the Nazis for two years along with her family. Her diary was published two years after the war by her father and provides a unique look at the personal life, thoughts, and feelings of a young girl whose life was thrown into turmoil at the height of World War II.

Hiroshima by John Hersey (1946)

Hiroshima was published just one year after World War II, but the horrific and saddening stories it features are timeless. John Hersey's unsettling book follows the lives of six Japanese civilians who survived the dropping of the atomic bomb on Hiroshima. This short book delves deep into their lives before and after the blast, revealing the unfathomable horrors caused by nuclear weapons.

The Longest Day by Cornelius Ryan (1959)

The Longest Day is one of the earliest in-depth works published about the D-Day invasion. Cornelius Ryan based his iconic book on interviews with more than 1,000 survivors and eye-witnesses. His now-legendary text reached the big screen when it was adapted into a major motion picture of the same name in 1962. The term *The Longest Day* has remained synonymous with the invasion of Normandy ever since. While the movie does not retain the same level of historical accuracy as the book, it is still among the classic must-see World War II flicks.

Stalingrad: The Fateful Siege: 1942–1943 by Antony Beevor (1998)

Antony Beevor's *Stalingrad* is a brilliant narrative history that illustrates the horror and magnitude of the battle on both sides. It maintains a balance of scholarly knowledge and captivating firsthand stories, combining them to become arguably the definitive book on Stalingrad, a turning point in the history of modern warfare. The book's graphic descriptions of war may not be for everyone, but the rawness is what distinguishes this informative and sobering read.

With the Old Breed: At Peleliu and Okinawa by E. B. Sledge (1981)

Written by a veteran of the war, *With the Old Breed* remains one of the most acclaimed World War II memoirs. Eugene Sledge's raw account of combat as a U.S. marine in the Pacific is based on notes he kept tucked away in a pocket-size Bible while fighting at Peleliu and Okinawa. Sledge's memoirs were later adapted into part of *The Pacific* (2010), a stunning miniseries produced by HBO. Both are highly recommended.

REFERENCES

Ambrose, Stephen E. *Band of Brothers: E Company, 506th Regiment, 101st Airborne from Normandy to Hitler's Eagle's Nest*. New York: Simon & Schuster, 2004.

———. *D Day: June 6, 1944: The Climactic Battle of World War II*. New York: Simon & Schuster, 1995.

"American Isolationism in the 1930s." Office of the Historian, U.S. Department of State, n.d. History.State.gov /milestones/1937-1945/american-isolationism.

"American Occupation of Japan, 1945–1952, The." Asia for Educators: Columbia University, n.d. AFE.EAsia.Columbia .edu/special/japan_1900_occupation.htm.

"Anzio—The Invasion That Almost Failed." Imperial War Museums, n.d. IWM.org.uk/history/anzio-the -invasion-that-almost-failed.

"B-29, The." PBS. Public Broadcasting Service, n.d. PBS.org /wgbh/americanexperience/features/flygirls-b-29.

Balkoski, Joseph. *Omaha Beach: D-Day, June 6, 1944*. Mechanicsburg, PA: Stackpole Books, 2006.

"Battle for Crete, The." New Zealand History, n.d. NZHistory .govt.nz/war/the-battle-for-crete/overview.

"Battle of Guadalcanal, The." National World War II Museum, New Orleans, August 5, 2019. NationalWW2Museum .org/war/articles/battle-guadalcanal.

"Battle of the Atlantic." Naval History and Heritage Command, n.d. History.Navy.mil/browse-by-topic

/wars-conflicts-and-operations/world-war-ii/1942
/atlantic.html.

"Battle of the Atlantic, The." Veterans Affairs Canada, January 27, 2020. Veterans.GC.ca/eng/remembrance/history/historical-sheets/atlantic.

Beevor, Antony. *Ardennes 1944: The Battle of the Bulge.* New York: Penguin Books, 2016.

———. *The Fall of Berlin, 1945.* New York: Viking, 2003.

———. *Stalingrad: The Fateful Siege: 1942–1943.* New York: Penguin Books, 1999.

Biggs, Jason. *Skies of World War II: Courage, Battle and Victory in the Air.* New York: Chartwell Books, 2014.

Bishop, Chris. *The Encyclopedia of Weapons of World War II.* New York: MetroBooks, 2002.

Bishop, Chris, and Adam Warner. *German Campaigns of World War II.* Edison, NJ: Chartwell Books, 2001.

Blair, Clay. *Hitler's U-Boat War: The Hunted, 1942–1945.* New York: Random House, 1998.

"Bombings of Hiroshima and Nagasaki—1945." Atomic Heritage Foundation, June 5, 2014. AtomicHeritage.org/history/bombings-hiroshima-and-nagasaki-1945.

Bosworth, R. J. B. *Mussolini's Italy: Life Under the Fascist Dictatorship, 1915–1945.* New York: Penguin Books, 2007.

Caddick-Adams, Peter. *Snow & Steel: The Battle of the Bulge, 1944–45.* Oxford, UK: Oxford University Press, 2014.

Craig, William. *Enemy at The Gates: The Battle for Stalingrad.* Old Saybrook, CT: Konecky & Konecky, 1973.

Darman, Peter. *World War II: Stats and Facts.* New York: Fall River Press, 2009.

Dimbleby, Jonathan. *The Battle of the Atlantic: How the Allies Won the War.* Oxford, UK: Oxford University Press, 2016.

Editors of *Encyclopædia Britannica.* "Battle of the Bulge." *Encyclopædia Britannica,* September 23, 2020. Britannica.com/event/Battle-of-the-Bulge.

———. "Pacific War." *Encyclopædia Britannica*, n.d. Britannica
.com/topic/Pacific-War.

———. "Siege of Leningrad." *Encyclopædia Britannica*,
September 1, 2020. Britannica.com/event
/Siege-of-Leningrad.

"End of World War II and the Division of Europe, The." Center
for European Studies at University of North Carolina at
Chapel Hill, n.d. Europe.UNC.edu/the-end-of-wwii
-and-the-division-of-europe.

"Firebombing of Tokyo." History.com. A&E Television Networks, November 16, 2009, last updated March 6, 2020.
History.com/this-day-in-history/firebombing-of-tokyo.

Frank, Richard B. *Guadalcanal: The Definitive Account of the
Landmark Battle*. New York: Penguin Books, 1992.

Freeman, Roger A. *The Mighty Eighth: A History of the Units,
Men and Machines of the US 8th Air Force*. London:
Cassell, 2000.

Gellately, Robert. *The Oxford Illustrated History of the Third
Reich*. Oxford, UK: Oxford University Press, 2018.

Guderian, Heinz. *Panzer Leader*. Cambridge, MA:
Da Capo, 2002.

Hammel, Eric. *Iwo Jima*. St. Paul, MN: Zenith Press, 2006.

———. *War in the Western Pacific: The U.S. Marines
in the Marianas, Peleliu, Iwo Jima, and Okinawa,
1944–1945*. Minneapolis, MN: Zenith Press, 2014.

Hastings, Max. *Inferno: The World at War, 1939–1945*. New
York: Vintage Books, 2012.

"History of the Marshall Plan." George C. Marshall Foundation,
n.d. MarshallFoundation.org/marshall/the-marshall-plan
/history-marshall-plan.

History.com Editors. "Pearl Harbor." History.com. A&E Television Networks, October 29, 2009, last updated February
21, 2020. History.com/topics/world-war-ii/pearl-harbor.

Holland, James. *The Allies Strike Back, 1941–1943*. New York:
Grove Press, 2018.

———. *The Battle of Britain: Five Months That Changed History; May–October 1940*. New York: St. Martin's, 2011.

"Iwo Jima and Okinawa: Death at Japan's Doorstep." National World War II Museum, New Orleans, July 10, 2017. NationalWW2Museum.org/war/articles/iwo-jima -and-okinawa-death-japans-doorstep.

Jane's Fighting Ships of World War II. New York: Military Press, 1989.

Jasper, Joy Waldron. *The USS Arizona*. New York: St. Martin's Press, 2001.

Kagan, Neil, and Stephen G. Hyslop. "The Battle of Berlin Was the Soviet Victory That Ended World War II." *National Geographic*, May 7, 2020. NationalGeographic.com /history/magazine/2020/05-06/soviet-victory -battle-berlin-finished-nazi-germany.

Kershaw, Ian. *Hitler: A Biography*. New York: W. W. Norton, 2010.

MacMillan, Margaret, and Richard Holbrooke. *Paris 1919: Six Months That Changed the World*. New York: Random House, 2002.

Mann, Dr. Chris. *Great Battles of World War II*. Bath, UK: Parragon, 2017.

Marine Corps History Division. "World War II Marine Corps Chronology 1941–1946," n.d. USMCU.edu /Research/Marine-Corps-History-Division /Research-Tools-Facts-and-Figures /Chronologies-of-the-Marine-Corps /World-War-II-1941-1945.

"Marshall Plan, 1948." U.S. Department of State, n.d. History.state.gov/milestones/1945-1952/marshall-plan.

McEnery, Jim. *Hell in the Pacific: A Marine Rifleman's Jour- ney From Guadalcanal to Peleliu*. New York: Simon & Schuster, 2013.

McNab, Chris. *Hitler's Armies: A History of the German War Machine, 1939–45*. Oxford, UK: Osprey Pub., 2011.

"Occupation and Reconstruction of Japan, 1945–52."
U.S. Department of State, n.d. History.State.gov
/milestones/1945-1952/japan-reconstruction.

Overy, R. J. *Why the Allies Won*. New York: W. W.
Norton, 1997.

"Paris Peace Conference and the Treaty of Versailles,
The." U.S. Department of State, n.d. History.State.gov
/milestones/1914-1920/paris-peace.

Parker, Matthew. *Monte Cassino: The Hardest Fought Battle
of World War II*. New York: Anchor Books, 2005.

"Path to Pearl Harbor, The." National World War II Museum,
New Orleans, June 22, 2017. NationalWW2Museum.org
/war/articles/path-pearl-harbor.

Perret, Geoffrey. *Winged Victory: The Army Forces in World
War II*. New York: Random House, 1993.

Prange, G. W. *Miracle at Midway*. London: McGraw-Hill, 1982.

Raaen, John C., Jr. *Intact: A First-Hand Account of the D-Day
Invasion from a 5th Rangers Company Commander*.
St. Louis, MO: Reedy Press, 2012.

Reid, Anna. *Leningrad: The Epic Siege of World War II,
1941–1944*. London: Bloomsbury, 2012.

Reynolds, Harley. *How I Survived the Three First Wave
Invasions: North Africa, Sicily and Omaha Beach*. Minneapolis, MN: Mill City Press, 2008.

Ryan, Cornelius. *The Longest Day, The Classic Epic of D-Day,
June 6, 1944*. New York: Simon & Schuster, 1994.

Saaler, Sven. "Nationalism and History in Contemporary
Japan." Asia-Pacific Journal: Japan Focus, October 15,
2016. APJJF.org/2016/20/Saaler.html.

Salisbury, Harrison E. *The 900 Days: The Siege of Leningrad*.
Cambridge, MA: Da Capo, 2003.

Scott, James. *Rampage: MacArthur, Yamashita, and the
Battle of Manila*. New York: W. W. Norton, 2019.

Shirer, William L. *The Rise and Fall of the Third Reich: A History of Nazi Germany*. New York: Simon & Schuster, 2011.

Showalter, Dennis E. *Armor and Blood: The Battle of Kursk; The Turning Point of World War II*. New York: Random House, 2013.

Sledge, E. B. *With the Old Breed at Peleliu and Okinawa*. New York: Presidio Press, 2007.

Smith, Larry. *Iwo Jima: World War II Veterans Remember the Greatest Battle of the Pacific*. New York: W. W. Norton, 2009.

Snyder, Timothy. *Bloodlands: Europe Between Hitler and Stalin*. New York: Basic Books, 2012.

"Solomons Campaign: Guadalcanal." Naval History and Heritage Command, November 4, 2020. History .Navy.mil/browse-by-topic/wars-conflicts-and -operations/world-war-ii/1942/guadalcanal.html.

Soucy, Robert. "Fascism." *Encyclopædia Britannica*, November 4, 2020. Britannica.com/topic/fascism.

Stokes, Bruce. "70 Years after Hiroshima, Opinions Have Shifted on Use of Atomic Bomb." Pew Research Center, August 4, 2015. PewResearch.org/fact-tank/2015 /08/04/70-years-after-hiroshima-opinions -have-shifted-on-use-of-atomic-bomb.

"Struggle for North Africa, 1940–43, The." National Army Museum, n.d. NAM.AC.uk/explore /struggle-north-africa-1940-43.

Toland, John. *The Rising Sun: The Decline and Fall of the Japanese Empire, 1936–1945*. New York: Random House, 2003.

Ullrich, Volker. *Hitler: Downfall, 1939–1945*. Translated by Jefferson S. Chase. New York: Alfred A. Knopf, 2020.

United States Holocaust Memorial Museum. "Allied Military Operations in North Africa." Holocaust Encyclopedia, n.d. encyclopedia.USHMM.org/content/en/article /allied-military-operations-in-north-africa.

———. "Blitzkrieg (Lightning War)." Holocaust Encyclopedia, n.d. encyclopedia.USHMM.org/content/en/article/blitzkrieg-lightning-war.

———. "Introduction to the Holocaust." Holocaust Encyclopedia, n.d. encyclopedia.USHMM.org/content/en/article/introduction-to-the-holocaust.

———. "Invasion of Poland, Fall 1939." Holocaust Encyclopedia, May 30, 2019. encyclopedia.USHMM.org/content/en/article/invasion-of-poland-fall-1939.

———. "Liberation of Nazi Camps." Holocaust Encyclopedia, n.d. encyclopedia.USHMM.org/content/en/article/liberation-of-nazi-camps?series=89.

———. "Nuremberg Trials, The." Holocaust Encyclopedia, January 5, 2018. encyclopedia.USHMM.org/content/en/article/the-nuremberg-trials.

Vergun, David. "Remembering the Battle of Okinawa." U.S. Department of Defense, April 1, 2020. Defense.gov/Explore/Features/Story/Article/2130718/remembering-the-battle-of-okinawa.

———. "Strategic Bombing Matured Quickly During World War II." U.S. Department of Defense, October 22, 2019. defense.gov/Explore/Features/story/Article/1995480/strategic-bombing-matured-quickly-during-wwii.

Wagner, Margaret E., and David M. Kennedy. *The Library of Congress World War II Companion*. New York: Simon & Schuster, 2007.

Wallace, Chris, and Mitch Weiss. *Countdown 1945: The Extraordinary Story of the Atomic Bomb and the 116 Days That Changed the World*. New York: Avid Reader Press/Simon & Schuster, 2020.

Ward, Geoffrey C., Ken Burns, and Lynn Novick. *The War: An Intimate History, 1941–1945*. New York: A.A. Knopf, 2007.

Weinberg, Gerhard L. *A World at Arms: A Global History of World War II*. Cambridge, UK: Cambridge University Press, 2010.

"What Was the Battle of Crete?" Imperial War Museums, n.d. IWM.org.uk/history/what-was-the-battle-of-crete.

"What You Need to Know About the Dunkirk Evacuations." Imperial War Museums, n.d. IWM.org.uk/history /what-you-need-to-know-about-the-dunkirk -evacuations.

INDEX

R

Radio direction finding (RDF), 29

"Rape of Nanking," 9

Reichstag fire, 4, 5

Reparations, 2

Ribbentrop, Joachim von, 13

Rommel, Erwin, 71, 74, 76, 77, 88

Roosevelt, Franklin D., 10, 31, 55, 109, 110, 111

Rosenthal, Joe, 113

Royal Air Force (RAF), 28–29

Russia. See Soviet Union

S

Sedan, Battle of, 21

Selassie, Haile, 8

Shigemitsu, Mamoru, 129

Soviet Union
  alliance with Germany, 11–13
  Battle of Berlin, 101–104, 103
  Battle of Kursk, 46–49, 48
  Battle of Moscow, 37–38
  Battle of Stalingrad, 42–46, 43
  Operation Barbarossa, 34–36, 35
  postwar occupation of Germany, 126–127
  post–World War I, 2
  Second Battle of Kharkov, 41–42
  Siege of Leningrad, 38–40

Spain, 78

Speer, Albert, 131

Spruance, Raymond, 117

Stalin, Joseph, 34, 42, 133

Stalingrad, Battle of, 42–46, 43

Student, Kurt, 72–73

Submarines, 25–27

Sudetenland, 12

Suez Canal, 70

T

T-34 tank, 47

Tanks, 47, 75

Third Reich, 6

Timoshenko, Semyon, 41–42

Tojo, Hideki, 62

Toyoda, Soemu, 62

Treaty of Versailles, 2, 3, 11, 13, 14, 25

Truman, Harry S., 111, 119, 130

Truscott, Lucian, 84

Tuskegee Airmen, 134

Twain, Mark, 135

Type VII U-boats, 27

U

U-boats, 25–27

Umezu, Yoshijiro, 129

Union of Soviet Socialist Republics (USSR). See Soviet Union

United States
  atomic bombing of Hiroshima and Nagasaki, 119–122, 120
  Battle of Iwo Jima, 111–114, 112
  Battle of Leyte Gulf, 63–65, 64
  Battle of Luzon, 66–67
  Battle of Midway, 57–60, 58
  Battle of Okinawa, 117–119
  Battle of the Coral Sea, 56
  Battle of the Philippine Sea, 61–62
  bombing of Tokyo, 115–116
  Guadalcanal campaign, 60–61

ACKNOWLEDGMENTS

The world is a better place thanks to the men and women who made immeasurable sacrifices during World War II, and I am personally indebted to the ones who have graced me with their stories of heroism, bravery, and sacrifice. Thank you to these compelling storytellers. To my parents, I am eternally grateful for the inspiration and guidance you have given me. Through life's many challenges, you've remained steadfast and molded me into the person I am today. Thank you to my kind and generous brother, who continues to find his path in life while being a pillar of support; and my family, who have always embraced my passion with love, patience, and encouragement. To the incredible people I've had the privilege to meet around the world, thank you for sharing your culture and being a part of my journey. Finally, I'd like to express my sincere gratitude to the wonderful publishing team at Callisto Media for understanding the importance of learning about history and making this book a reality. It is my hope that this body of work will serve to educate and inspire generations to come.

ABOUT THE AUTHOR

Benjamin Mack-Jackson is an author, a documentary filmmaker, a historian, and, most importantly, a storyteller, capturing and preserving the memories of the world's last surviving World War II veterans. As the founder of the nonprofit organization WWII Veterans History Project, Benjamin dedicates his time to capturing untold stories of service and sacrifice. His acclaimed work has made an impact across the globe.

NOTES

NOTES

NOTES

NOTES

NOTES

_____

_____

_____

_____

_____

_____

_____

_____

_____

_____

_____

_____

_____

_____

_____

_____

_____

_____

_____

_____

_____

NOTES

NOTES

NOTES